CHOOSE YOUR WINE IN 7 SECONDS

CHOOSE YOUR WINE IN 7 SECONDS

Instantly Understand Any Wine With Confidence

UNIVERSE

CONTENTS

INTRODUCTION

MAKING WINE EASY

Are you one of those people who spends no more than one minute selecting their cheese or fruit and vegetables at the market, yet linger at least six minutes in bewilderment looking at wine shelves, and sometimes leave empty-handed? Consult this handy guide and you'll soon be finding your way around the wine section with the greatest of ease.

If you're like most people, you probably buy your wine at a local wine store or supermarket. Smaller supermarkets often merely categorize the bottles by the major types: reds, whites, rosés, sparkling, and sweet. Larger stores think they'll help you by giving a profusion of references and adding the names of the regions to the shelves: Bordeaux, Beaujolais, and more. But, true novice that you are, you have no idea what these names mean.

Does Bordeaux have a taste? How about Napa Valley? The wine section is like the shelves in a bookstore: the more titles there are, the better they are. Book lovers love to lose themselves among them, but more infrequent readers ask the bookseller for advice. The equivalent of a bookseller is a wine store manager or a sommelier . . . not someone you'll often find in a supermarket.

ANOTHER BOOK ABOUT WINE?

The dictionary definition of wine is simple: a beverage resulting from the total or partial alcoholic fermentation of grapes or the juice from grapes. Yet so many shoppers feel confused when they have to choose a wine. Why is it such a complex matter?

A DIZZYING ARRAY OF NAMES AND REFERENCES

Firstly, wine comes from a wide range of different sources, including:
- Wine-growing estates: chateaux, sometimes historical and prestigious, owned or managed by bigwigs, or vineyards run by unpretentious artisanal vintners;
- Cooperatives;
- Wine merchants.

Not to mention that the world of wine is also the playing field of multinationals.

Next, a wine does not only owe its fame to a brand, but also (and often) to a geographical area. This may be a large region, a small county, or sometimes even a tiny hamlet. Bordeaux, Champagne, Margaux, Chablis, Châteauneuf-du-Pape are all names that designate regions or villages. And alongside these famous references, there are hundreds of others, with about 400 appellations in France alone, and thousands of wines worldwide, such as Mendoza (Argentina) and Marlborough (New Zealand) to mention only two. Some people can sniff their way effortlessly through the complicated geography of wine. Others manage with less ease.

COMING TO GRIPS WITH CATEGORIES AND HIERARCHIES

Over the past few decades, New World wines have brought new names to wine labels, with names of varietals, or grape varieties. Chardonnay or Sauvignon? Merlot or Cabernet? To choose, you need to know about them. And there are further complications: you may have a vague idea of all those abbreviations, but what do all the hierarchical levels and categories refer to? For example, in France, there is the AOC/AOP classification; the *vins de pays* (the locally produced small labels that don't mention a domain name); the IGP label (*Indication géographique protégée*, or Protected Geographical Indication); and Vin de France. What are these categories? And what are the differences in color of wine: red wine, white wine, rosé wine ... and let's not forget yellow wine and even orange wine. When it's in your mouth, what does it taste like? Pricing is even more complex. Why does the Bordeaux region produce wines that cost $5 and others that cost $500?

In short, wine brings you into the world of labeling, in every sense of the word. Obscure references, a vocabulary for the cognoscenti, and under all this, hides a range of aromas and tastes meant to be drunk over a range of periods. This book reduces the best-known appellations to 300 names, and the 300 names to four types and ten categories. For each wine, similar wines will be indicated. Experts love to discuss the minute differences between wines, but so that you can be more efficient, we will teach you about the similarities. An oversimplification? For sure. But you can't deny that it's useful!

HOW TO USE THIS BOOK

We have selected 300 wines from the thousands of wines available on the market, and described them for you with the fewest possible words.

Name of the wine:
(in most cases, these are protected or designated appellations, see page 18)

Wine category:
the type of wine

Description in two words: giving you an idea of its distinctive characteristics

Aromas of the wine in pictograms: red fruit, spices, etc. (see page 210)

Price range (may vary):

$: under $10
$$: $10-17
$$$: $17-35
$$$$: $35-60
$$$$$: $60+

Mouthfeel: Firmness, heat, acidity

Suggestions for food pairings

Serving temperature

Best time to drink

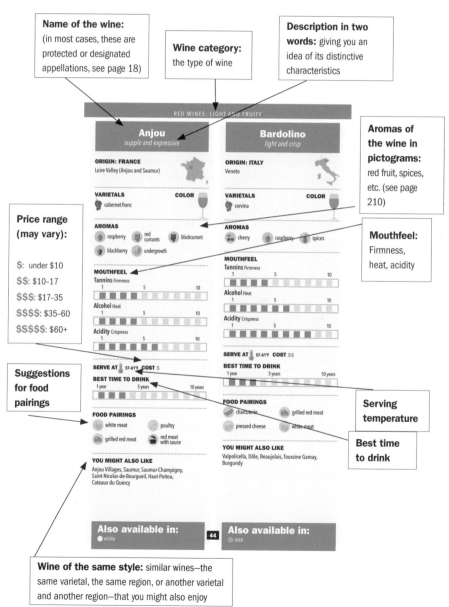

Wine of the same style: similar wines—the same varietal, the same region, or another varietal and another region—that you might also enjoy

WHERE TO BUY YOUR WINE

It's never been so easy to buy wine: supermarkets, independent retailers selling in stores or online, wine fairs, auction sales, all mean wine is readily available. And the Internet has changed the game, broadening the offer and increasing your opportunities to acquire wine. Each sales channel has its pros and cons—it all depends on your priorities.

BUYING ONLINE

Online sales of wine are exploding. The Internet could even be considered the largest wine store in the world.

Pros

Praticality: Order from home, choose an assortment of wines, home delivery.

A wide-ranging offer: You can buy wines from online wine sellers, virtual stores, winemakers, wine merchants, cooperatives, major stores, and traditional wine stores, magazines and wine guides.

Comparing prices: easy.

Cons

Information: Confusing or absent altogether.

Shipping costs and delivery periods: You may be in for a nasty surprise, so read the fine print before ordering.

Seller reliability: You can't necessarily count on your seller being reliable, so do your research, online and in the specialized press, before placing your order.

THE LOCAL WINE SELLER

Wine retailers, often with stores in city centers, visit the wineries to stock their shelves. Wine selling franchises, however, are part of a chain of stores and get their inventory from a central distributor.

The Franchised Wine Seller

PROS

Advice, just like other retailers

CONS

Fewer interesting bottles, because these stores are organized like supermarkets

Pros

Advice: Independent wine sellers are often true aficionados.

Tasting: These sellers are often keen to organize wine tastings.

Original vintages: These are places to make discoveries–wines from small estates, organic wines, and sometimes, interesting natural wines.

Cons

Cost: Prices are often higher than in supermarkets because these wine sellers buy limited quantities of wine.

Choice: Some wine sellers favor the wine-producing regions they like best to the detriment of others

WINE CLUBS

Wine clubs are often organized by wine merchants or independent sellers.

Pros

Opportunity: A chance to become acquainted with unusual wines, as well as quality wines, without hunting around too much.

Cons

Selection: What's on offer may well be limited.

Auction Sales

PROS

- Old vintages and rare classified growths
- Online bidding now possible

CONS

- Bottle storage: be sure to find out what condition the bottles are in (level of wine in the bottle); how they've been stored; their background. Call on a specialist.
- Major deposit required: bids are usually made for lots, and the legendary wines on auction are often very expensive.

BUYING AT A WINE ESTATE

Buying wine at an estate takes time, but affords real pleasure to the wine lover, providing an opportunity to meet the wine growers, discover new wines, and learn about winemaking directly in a friendly environment.

Learning about wine: Someone is there to talk to you about their work and their wines.

Learning about a region and its landscapes that may well be new for you: A fun way of learning geography.

An opportunity to follow the evolution of a wine, vintage after vintage.

Cons

Wine prices may well not be any lower when sold directly, as the wine producer is careful not to compete with their other clients (the wine merchants).

Distance, and finding the vineyard out in the country.

Opening hours and availability of the wine producer: You may have to make an appointment.

Pros

Tasting: Tasting a wine before you buy it is the ideal way of buying. Note that we say "taste"—this implies spitting out!

WINE FAIRS

Wine makers regularly come into the city to meet their clients, and fairs give wine lovers a chance to see a wide range of products.

Pros

Tasting: There's no better way of buying than tasting beforehand.

Learning about wine: The winemakers attending are happy to talk about their work and wines.

Cons

It's hard to find your way through a large wine fair: Prepare for your visit and don't go at the busiest times.

SUPERMARKETS

Nearly 80 percent of all wines are bought in supermarkets. Because so many purchasers are far from both city centers and wine estates, they may well have no other choice.

Pros

Practicality: All the components of a meal can be bought in one place.

Wide-ranging choice: About 800 different products are available in supermarkets.

Competitive pricing: Supermarket chains buy large volumes and have a negotiating edge.

Wine events: Every year in September and October, supermarkets have special offers with higher-range wines than their usual stock. In spring, they highlight wines for summer drinking (rosés, dry whites, and fruity reds in particular).

Convenience: Sometimes interactive terminals and apps are available for customers.

Cons

No advice given, except sometimes during the periods of special wine events.

Only the most cursory of information on the shelves: (color and type of wines, sometimes the regions are given).

The accent is on large, constant producing areas: Regions with small estates (Burgundy, Alsace, Corsica, etc.) do not have a notable presence, and you'll find many merchant-blended wines and wines from cooperatives, with few high-end wines, except for the periods of the wine fairs.

Retailers' brands

These are the labels of supermarkets, who generally obtain their wine from merchants and cooperatives. So their wines are entry-level products whose provenance is often indicated in small print on the back label (see page 17).

BOTTLES AND THEIR CONTENTS

No, we're not going to start cluttering your mind by explaining that the Nebuchadnezzar contains fifteen liters and the equivalent of twenty bottles of Champagne, and the slew of other bottles with names of kings that go almost back to Methuselah. The names are hard to pronounce and the bottles, difficult to handle. It's far more useful to take a look at the containers that we can see every time we go to the store. The bottles illustrated below give us pointers about their contents. Here's how:

Bordeaux

Distinctive features: Cylindrical shape with high shoulders, ideal for retaining the sediments found in tannic wines.
Regions: Bordeaux, South West France, Provence, Languedoc-Roussillon (sometimes), and other regions that produce tannic wines in both the Old and New Worlds.

Burgundy

Distinctive features: Sloping shoulders.
Regions: Burgundy, Beaujolais, Rhône Valley, Center of the Loire (Sancerre), and for Pinot Noir and Chardonnay wines of the New World.

Champagne

Distinctive features: The bottle is heavy enough to withstand the pressure of the gas produced by the bubbles when it's opened. More often than not, the bottle is dark-colored because light affects this type of wine (and the case is useful).
Regions: All regions that produce sparkling wines.

Muscadet

Distinctive features: Tall, slender bottle.
Regions: The regions around Nantes, Western France. Wines from Anjou are similarly bottled.

Clavelin from the Jura

Distinctive features: This squat shape, that contains only 62 cl (22 oz.), is used exclusively for *vin jaune* (yellow wine) from a single region in France.
Regions: Jura, Eastern France

Alsace

Distinctive feature: This is known in French as the *flute d'Alsace*, and is the official, exclusive type for wines from Alsace.

Provençale

Distinctive features: A shape that tapers in the middle. One of the models used to bottle wines from Provence.
Region: Provence

Signs for Wines

Certain bottle shapes may only be used for wine from certain regions (such as Alsace and Jura) and appellations, but nowadays, winemakers enjoy increasing freedom in their choice of bottle. The area where these bottles are used are vast, often larger than the delimited region.

Corks

Synthetic: Little elasticity and hard to handle. For wines that don't wait.

Agglomerated cork: Not high quality; for wines to drink young.

One-piece natural cork: For good-quality wines; must be very long for wines that are going to be cellared for long aging. Good elasticity, but with a risk of imparting a corky taste.

Diam Corks: Made from cork granules using a patented technology that removes the molecules that cause bad taste from the cork.

Screw caps: Widely used, sometimes for whites and wines that are meant to be drunk young. Prevents corked wine and the use of a corkscrew.

The most widely found bottle shapes

0.2 liter: quart

0.25 liter: chopine

0.37 liter: *fillette,* or half-bottle, often found in restaurants

0.5 liter: practical for sweet wines that are drunk in small quantities

0.75 liter: standard bottle

1 liter: for entry-range wine

1.5 liters: magnum, ideal for cellaring

Larger formats: double-magnum (3 liters), Jeroboam, etc.

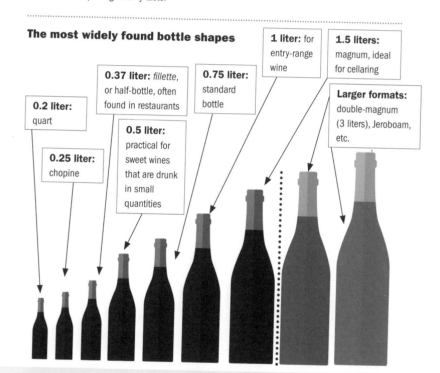

Bag-in-Box

What's this? The packaging comprises a flexible bag of multi-layered plastic, a cardboard box, a handle for transport, and a tap. The tap prevents air from getting in, and the flexible bag retracts after wine is served, so that it doesn't oxidize.

Pros:
• Long storage—six weeks after opening
• Ideal for drinking small quantities every day, and for self-service buffets

Cons:
You'll only found entry-level wines, and perhaps mid-range wines (regional appellations and PGIs)

READING THE LABEL

The label is the wine's visiting card, its certificate of authenticity, and also its advertising. Labels are often complex, with mandatory information, optional details, plus whatever the producer sees fit to add. If you can decode the label, you'll get an initial idea of the contents of the bottle, even though wine always has surprises in store for us.

MANDATORY LABELING

1. Name and address of the bottler, who is responsible for the wine.

2. Batch or vat number.

3. Volume: volume of bottle contents.

4. Alcohol content: Gives the percentage of alcohol in relation to the volume of liquid contained in the bottle.

5. Warning for pregnant women.

6. Contains sulfites: This information must be provided if the wine contains 10 mg per liter or more, because allergic reactions are possible.

7. Wine ranking: Terms that indicate the ranking of the wine in an official hierarchy of quality. For example, in France: the AOC/AOP(*Appellation d'origine controlee/protégée*), PGI (Protected Geographical Indication), Vin de France.

8. Country of origin.

OPTIONAL INFORMATION

9. Name of the estate, château, or brand: Although not mandatory, you'll always find this, giving the identity of the wine and the producer.

10. Vintage: the year the grapes are harvested has an impact on the quality of the wine. Keep in mind that 15% of the wine within a bottle may have been harvested during a different year.

Other useful information

The varietals (grape varieties) used to make the wine. For example, Gamays are often lively and fruity, while Cabernet Sauvignons are well-structured. Information regarding varietals is not given for wines of very prestigious appellations, such as Montrachet, which is made with the Chardonnay grape.

Place name (often a hamlet) where the wine is made: This is often given for wines from Burgundy and Alsace, for example.

Ranking: for a Bordeaux wine, for example

Medal won: the wine may have been awarded a medal in a competition

Information on the type of wine or the way it was produced, for example: Barrel aged; sweet; *vin gris* (a rosé wine is made by draining off the clear juice from the crushed red grapes); a crémant or a sparkling wine made using the *méthode traditionnelle* (the method used to make Champagne also makes for quality sparkling wines); *vendanges tardives* (late harvest), a sweet wine made from overripe grapes, typically in Alsace; *sélection de grains nobles* (a sweet wine made from wines affected by noble rot).

The name of the lot (cuvee): winemakers often give a name to their wine that may identify them and sometimes gives other information, which may refer to a family member or vineyard.

Information on Sparkling Wines

It is mandatory to provide information concerning the sugar content: from the driest to the sweetest: brut nature, extra-brut, brut, extra-dry, demi-sec, and doux.

Turn the bottle to look on the other side

Increasingly, you'll find that labels say virtually nothing of interest. The label that you can see on the supermarket shelf has little information, and some–or even all– of the mandatory information, including the legal information, is on the back.

CHÂTEAU
DU GRAND VIN

APPELLATION BORDEAUX CONTRÔLÉE

2014

This wine, a harmonious blend of Merlot and Cabernet Sauvignon will pair well with poultry, roasted or grilled white and red meats, and pressed cheeses.

Serve at 62–64˚F

Age for 5 to 6 years

L1 Contains sulfites

Product of France

Certifié par Ecocert FR. BIO-01.

12.5% vol.   BOTTLED BY BOUTEILLE PAR SARL VINCENT LAVIGNE
CHÂTEAU DU GRAND VIN 33670 LA SAUVE   750 ML

THE CLASSIFICATION OF FRENCH WINES

Many wines owe their name and reputation to the place from where they originate. This is why "appellations" exist, and appellations are to be found worldwide today.

AOC (*Appellation d'origine contrôlée*), Controlled Designation of Origin: These wines make up the tip of the pyramid in the official hierarchy of French wines. They are also known as AOP (*Appellation d'origine protégée*).

· The initials AOC guarantee that the wine in the bottle is from a certain region (such as Bordeaux) and of a certain style.

· A geographical area delimited by the viticultural features of the terroir (characteristics given to a wine by the environment in which it is produced), including the ground, slope, and microclimate.

· Precise specifications concerning the varietal and the winery, explaining time-honored local techniques.

IGP (*Indication géographique protégée*): This is the European Union's new designation that replaces the former "Vin de Pays".

· This term always goes hand-in-hand with the name of a region, such as Pays d'Oc, Côtes de Gascogne, Côte Vermeille, and a delimited geographical that is often larger than the AOCs.

· The specifications are less stringent than for the AOC, with an often sizable list of varietals, and fewer cultural constraints in terms of the wine-making.

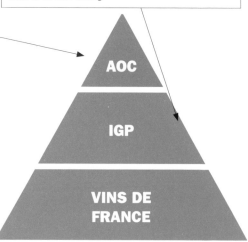

AOC

IGP

VINS DE FRANCE

In other countries

All wine-producing countries in the European Union have a similar classification system. Spain for example, has *Denominción de origen califacada*, *Denominción de origen* (DOC/DO), and *Vinos de la tierra*. In Italy, you will find *Denominazione di origine controllata e garantita* (DOCG), *Denominazione di origine controllata* (DOC), and *indicazione geografica tipica*. In the US, a wine labeled with an American viticultural area (AVA), indicates that at least 85% of the wine's grapes must come from that AVA (e.g. Napa Valley).

Vins de France approximately 7% of all wine produced in France, were formerly known as *vins de table*, table wines.

· The most basic category of wine production.

· France: refers to the provenance–the wine may be made from a mixture of varietals from several French vineyards.

· Few constraints on wine making: the only restrictions concern vinification techniques outlawed by the European Union.

· The wines may be standardized, off-specification, or craft wines.

THE APPELLATION HIERARCHY

In the major, well-established vineyards, such as those of Burgundy, the AOCs are ranked in a hierarchy, with the smallest and most prestigious at the apex of the pyramid.

What is a cru classé?

In the Bordeaux region, this refers to a château (a property or estate) that is listed in a classification system. In Burgundy and Alsace, a cru classé refers to a terroir that is delimited in terms of its quality (premier cru, grand cru).

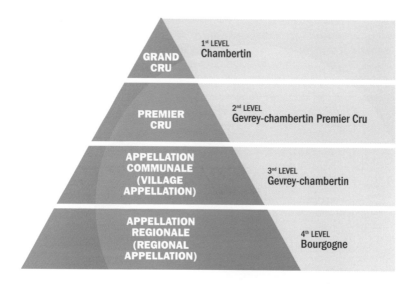

GRAND CRU	1st LEVEL Chambertin
PREMIER CRU	2nd LEVEL Gevrey-chambertin Premier Cru
APPELLATION COMMUNALE (VILLAGE APPELLATION)	3nd LEVEL Gevrey-chambertin
APPELLATION REGIONALE (REGIONAL APPELLATION)	4th LEVEL Bourgogne

ORGANIC WINE

Organic wine is wine made using organic farming methods and produced to meet certain precise specifications:

· In the vineyards, no synthetic chemical products are used such as insecticides or weed killers, and there are no GMOs.

· In European wineries, the vintner must respect specifications outlines by the EU. The dosage of sulfur is lower and certain practices are not authorized.

· In the US, requirements for organic wines are more strict; in order to bear the USDA Organic certification the wine must not have any added sulfites.

Natural Wine

This term indicates if the wine is organic and has no additives, or minimal additives (sulfur in particular). At the time of publication, no official specifications exist.

WINE PRICES

The finest wine (by which we mean a wine that is complex, one that bowls you over) is never cheap, but the wine that suits you best is not necessarily the most expensive. What determines the price of wine? Its scarcity, the prestige of the vineyard where it is produced, current trends, the quantities produced, and the techniques used to make it. And of course, marketing costs must also be factored in.

SCARCITY

In the more prestigious wine-producing areas, the smaller the size of the appellation area, the higher the cost of the wine. Let's compare the price of wines that have a Pomerol appellation with those of a regional Bordeaux appellation (see table below). However, there are also small-sized vineyards that produce very pleasant wines at reasonable prices. For example, the wines of the Aveyron region, such as the Marcillac, and the wines of the Savoy region. The reason? They are reputed to be *vins de terroir*—with a specific terroir.

	Pomerol	Generic Bordeaux (regional AOC)
Vineyard surface	2,175 acres (3.4 sq. miles)	278,000 acres/436.4 sq. miles (theoretically, the entire wine-producing area of the Bordeaux region)
Floor price range per vat	$18–$24 (€15–€20)	Under $6 (€5)
Ceiling price	$3,000–$3,600 (€2,500–€3,000) (Petrus) + than 90% for vats over $24 (€20)	($18–$24) to (€15–€20) 80% of the vats <€8

Wine Vintage (Year of Harvesting) and Price

The weather during the year of harvest plays a major role in the volume and quality of the grapes picked, influencing, most notably, the aging potential of the wine. The "vintage" factor mainly influences the price of wines for cellaring and prestigious wines.

PRESTIGE

Now let's compare Champagne and crémants, which are prepared using the same method.

	Champagne	Crémants
Floor price range	$13-$30 (€11-€25)	About $6 (€5)
Ceiling price range	> $2,355 (€2,000) for Krug Clos d'Ambonnay + than 80% for vats over $18 (€15)	$18-24 (€15-€20) (about 1%) 90% of the vats range between ($6) €5 and $13 (€11)

The renown of a wine influences the price of the land, which in turn impacts the price of wine. Crémants, for example, are produced in regions like Alsace, where land prices are lower than in the Champagne region.

	Champagne	Alsace
Current price per hectare (2.5 acres) (2013)	$1,197,750 (€1,000,000)	$122,170 (€102,000) Bas Rhin department
	Pomerol	**Bordeaux (regional AOC)**
Current price per hectare (2.5 acres) (2013)	$1,197,750 (€1,000,000)	$18,000 (€15,000)

Source : Légifrance

MARKETING AND POSITIONING

The positioning of a wine on the market influences the way in which it is marketed and thus its price. A prestigious Champagne producer, for instance, will target a well-off clientele worldwide to sell their special cuvées. This implies that the marketing budget is very high in terms of both packaging (bottles and luxury cases) and communication (special events, sponsorship, website, etc.). Independent producers who sell the product of their (probably small) estate to a more limited clientele, often faithful buyers, spend less on marketing and communication and thus their prices are lower.

WINE PRODUCTION METHODS

The methods used also have a direct impact on the price of a bottle.

Prestigious wines

· Painstaking work on the vines, with rigorous sorting if rainfall is particularly heavy in any given years
· Equipment in the winery (frequently modernized, high tech material)
· Long wine aging (price of barrels, storage of at least 16 to 18 months in a winery for the top Bordeaux, bottles rested in cellars for 15 months to 3 years minimum for Champagne)

Basic wines: For wines with no geographical provenance indicated, or entry-level bottles:

· Grapes are machine harvested
· Wines from different regions are blended
· Use of additives to correct the harvest and standardize the product

WINE PRICES: WHAT'S YOUR RANGE?

	$ A casual drink	$$ Enjoy with company	$$$ A gastronomical meal
RED WINES: LIGHT AND FRUITY	Anjou Bardolino Beaujolais	Sancerre Saint-Amour Valpolicella	Pinot Noir (Anderson Valley)
RED WINES: FLESHY AND FRUITY	Bordeaux Ruby Cabernet (California) Saumur-Champigny	Barbera d'Alba Graves Rioja (Crianza)	Pinot Noir (New Zealand) Saint-Joseph
RED WINES: POWERFUL AND BALANCED	Madiran	Cahors Douro Syrah (Hunter Valley)	Haut-Médoc (classified) Pommard Saint-Émilion Grand Cru
RED WINES: RIPE AND SPICY	Costières de Nîmes Côtes du Rhône Fitou Saint-Chinian	Bandol Gigondas Yecla	Châteauneuf-du-Pape Zinfandel (Sonoma Valley)
RED WINES: SWEET		Ruby Port	Tawny Port
ROSÉ WINES	Côtes de Provence Languedoc-Roussillon Rosé-d'Anjou	Navarra Côtes de Provence Bardolino Chiaretto	Côtes de Provence (the best known)
WHITE WINES: CRISP AND FRUITY	White Bordeaux Muscadet Sèvre et Maine Orvieto Vinho Verde	Alsace Riesling Chablis Pouilly-Fumé Sancerre Rueda Pinot Grigio	Chablis Grand Cru German Riesling Sauvignon Blanc (Marlborough)
WHITE WINES: FULL AND ROUND	White Burgundy Torrontès (Salta) Limoux Mâcon-Villages	Graves Chardonnay (Casablanca) Sherry Fino	Meursault Pinot Noir (Walker Bay) Vin Jaune
WHITE WINES: SWEET	Moscato (California)	Coteaux du Layon Monbazillac	Alsace *vendanges tardives* Sweet Riesling
SPARKLING WINES	German Sekt Clairette-de-Die Crémants Prosecco	Champagne (RM) Crémants Sparkling Shiraz	Champagne

	$$$$ High prestige	$$$$$ Legendary wines
RED WINES: **LIGHT AND FRUITY**		
RED WINES: **FLESHY AND FRUITY**	Chianti Classico (the best known)	
RED WINES: **POWERFUL AND** **BALANCED**	Côte-Rôtie Cabernet Sauvignon (Oakville) Pomerol	Saint-émilion Premier Grands Crus Classés Pomerol (the best known) Premier Crus Classés du Médoc (Pauillac, Pessac-Léognan...) Grands crus bourguignons
RED WINES: **RIPE AND SPICY**	Rioja (Gran Reserva) Priorat (the best known)	
RED WINES: SWEET	Vintage Port	Vintage Port
ROSÉ WINES		
WHITE WINES: **CRISP AND FRUITY**		
WHITE WINES: **FULL AND ROUND**	Condrieu Chardonnay (Santa Cruz Mountains) Pessac-Léognan Classé	Corton-Charlemagne Grand Cru Hermitage Meursault Premier Cru Montrachet
WHITE WINES: SWEET	Tokaj doux Quarts de Chaume Riesling (Mosel) Sauternes	Sauternes (Crus Classés)
SPARKLING WINES	Vintage Champagne	Champagne (prestige cuvées)

This table only provides a few examples. You need to know that many wines are available in several ranges, so you can find a Pomerol for less than $20, while a Petrus (Pomerol) is one of the most expensive wines in the world. The rating of the wine must also be factored in.

Making the right choice
- Find a suitable wine for the people and the event
- Got a legendary wine? Keep it as a gift for a dear one and/or a lover of the region or provenance of the wine
- An everyday wine? Serve it at a party or buffet
- Select a wine that pairs well with the dish you'll be serving (see page 35)

TASTING WINE

Tasting wine involves sight, smell, and then taste. Touch also comes in, as we perceive the temperature of the wine, the warmth of the alcohol, the astringency or texture of the tannins, and the gas in the sparkling wines. Even the sense of hearing contributes to the pleasure of the wine-drinking experience, when we hear the pop of the cork as it is pulled out or the fizzing of the bubbles in sparkling wines.

THE COLOR OF WINE

The color of wine, known as the *robe* in French, also provides information on its intensity and clarity. The hues of a wine give an indication of its age and its category. They are a result of the grape varietal (Syrah makes for red colored wines; Gamays are lighter in color); they also reveal how the wine has aged or changed (young reds have violet reflections; aged wines have brick-colored reflections; and young whites have green reflections that darken with aging). Sometimes, wine leaves "tears" (also known as "legs") on the sides of the glass, revealing the presence of glycerol, a viscous, sweet-tasting composite that gives wine its unctuousness, an impression that it is "fat."

Red wines: light and fruity

Young wines have violet-colored reflections

White wines: crisp and fruity and young white wines

Yellow green

Red wines: powerful and balanced

Young wines have violet-colored reflections

White wines: full and round

Straw yellow

Some sweet red wines and aged red wines

Brick-colored reflections

Sweet white wines and dry whites that are past their optimal age

Orangey yellow

Pink rosé wines

Almost red, strawberry pink

Gray rosé wines

Very pale pink with silvery reflections

THE NOSE OF WINE: THE AROMAS

When we talk of the "nose" of a wine, we are referring to the perfumes we perceive when we sniff the wine. When the glass is swirled, the wine is aerated and new aromas are revealed. Examining the nose sometimes also brings out defects, such as that most unacceptable of all: corked wine. Tasters identify aromas by analogy and group them into categories, including fruity aromas, floral, vegetal, spicy, and mineral (see page 26).

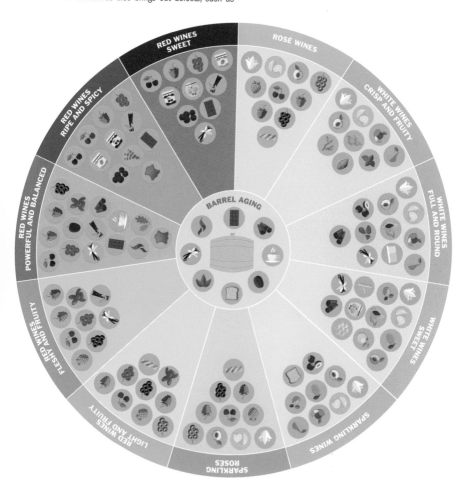

THE PRINCIPAL CATEGORIES OF AROMAS

Categories	Main aromas
Floral	White flowers (hawthorn, jasmine, honeysuckle); linden or lime trees, violet, rose, peony, iris, etc.
Fruity	Red fruit (cherry, raspberry, red currant, strawberry); black fruit (black currant, blackberry, blueberry, dark plums); white (apple, pear, quince, white peach); yellow fruit (yellow peach, apricot, Mirabelle plum); exotic fruit (mango, lychee, passion fruit, pineapple); nuts (hazelnut, walnut, almond); citrus (lemon, orange, grapefruit, mandarin oranges)
Vegetal	Grass, ferns, mint, boxwood, scrubland, forest undergrowth, mushroom
Spicy	Pepper, cinnamon, vanilla, licorice, clove, nutmeg, ginger
Balsamic	Resin, pine, turpentine, sandalwood
Animal	Meat, leather, game, musk, fur
Roasted	Aromas related to the action of fire: burned, roasted (coffee, cacao); smoked; toast; tobacco; caramel; dried hay
Mineral	Flintstone, graphite, gasoline, iodine
Pastry	Honey, brioche
Milky	Fresh butter, cream

MOUTHFEEL

It is in the mouth that the wine lover truly appreciates the qualities and harmony of a wine. Tasters break the perception of wine on the palate (a synonym for the mouth) into phases, the first one of which is the attack (the initial sensations), the second, the middle-range, mid palate, or evolution phase, and finally, the finish (the last sensations).

Wine on the palate must give an impression of balance between the flavors, chiefly: acidity, sweetness, bitterness, and, sometimes, saltiness.

Acidity, found in all wines, is clearly dominant in dry white wines that are crisp and fruity.

Sweetness is found only in sweet wines. Nevertheless, alcohol, which is nothing but sugar transformed through fermentation, gives an impression of roundness that is almost sweet, and sometimes warm.

Tannins are present in red wines, but to a lesser degree in reds that are light and fruity. They bring a slight bitterness (a grainy aspect) to young wines and a feeling of astringency, which leaves the mouth feeling dry. This is the reason why we allow well-structured, tannic wines to age: their tannins are smoothed out with time.

Flavors on the palate: Wine heats and spreads on the palate, and new aromas are perceived retro-nasally. If there are multiple aromas, we can talk of the complexity of the wine. If they last, we say it has length–all qualities that we seek out in a wine.

Keys to interpretation

For each of the 300 wines described in the chapters to follow, we have indicated a scale for the feelings of acidity, sweetness (for the sweet wines), alcohol (an impression of warmth), and the strength of the tannins of the red wines (firmness).

Tannins Firmness

1 5 10

THE VOCABULARY OF MOUTHFEEL

Degrees of acidity

Lack	Satisfactory			Excess
Flat, soft	Soft	Fresh, lively	Nervy	Green, biting, aggressive

A lively wine: Bourgogne Aligoté

Degrees of sweetness

Lack	Satisfactory			Excess
Dry	Soft, supple	Sweet	Liquoureux (slightly syrupy)	Heavy, thick, too syrupy

A sweet wine: Sauternes

Alcohol strength

Lack	Satisfactory			Excess
Weak, thin	Light	Generous, vinous	Powerful, warm, heady	Burning, alcoholic finish

A warm wine: Châteauneuf-du-Pape

Presence of tannins (red wines)

Lack	Satisfactory			Excess
Smooth, supple	Silky, velvety, mellow	Well-structured	Tannic, robust virile	Rustic, angular, rough, rasping astringent, drying, hard, acerbic

A tannic wine: Pauillac

WINE THE EASY WAY: TEN CATEGORIES

With over 400 appellations in France, approximately as many in Italy, at least sixty in Spain, not to mention all those of the New World, as well as the IGPs (*Indication géographique protégée*, the European Union's new designation for member states), the array is bewildering. In this book, we have divided wines into four types and ten categories. This may seem like over-simplification, and it's true that some appellations encompass several appellations according to precise terroirs, the personal touch of the wine producer, and the vintage. At some stage in the future, you'll enjoy delving further into the complexities of the table below. You'll have become a fine connoisseur, and will seek out the differences between wines of the same appellation, depending on which side of a road or a river they are grown.

WINE CATEGORIES: AN OVERVIEW

Category	Examples	Color	Dominant aromas	Balance (mouthfeel)
Red wines: light and fruity	Beaujolais Bardolino		Fruity and floral aromas	Strong presence of acidity (crispness)
Red wines: fleshy and fruity	Saumur-Champigny Carmenère from Chile		Fruity and floral aromas Spicy aromas (barrel aged)	Moderate presence of tannins
Red wines: powerful and balanced	Pauillac Cabernet-Sauvignon from Napa Valley		Fruity and floral aromas Spicy aromas (if barrel aged) Aromas of undergrowth	Strong presence of tannins (impression that wine has backbone)

Category	Examples	Color	Dominant aromas	Balance (mouthfeel)
Red wines: ripe and spicy	Châteauneuf-du-Pape Zinfandel from Sonoma Valley		Fruity and floral aromas Spicy aromas Aromas of undergrowth	Pronounced presence of alcohol
Red wines: sweet	Porto Banyuls	Varies according to the style (vintage or tawny	Vintage style Tawny style	Pronounced presence of alcohol and sugar
Rosé wines	Côtes de Provence Tavel		White wine aromas Red wine aromas	Pronounced presence of acidity (crispness), sometimes sweetness
White wines: crisp and fruity	Sancerre Rueda		Fruity and floral aromas Vegetal aromas Mineral aromas	Strong presence of acidity (crispness)

Category	Examples	Color	Dominant aromas	Balance (mouthfeel)
White wines: full and round	Meursault Soave		Fruity and floral aromas Spicy aromas Milky aromas Roasted aromas (barrel aged)	Acidity tempered by a certain presence of alcohol
White wines: sweet	Sauternes Alsace *vendanges tardives* Coteaux-du-Layon		Fruity and floral aromas (barrel aged)	Strong presences of sweetness (balanced by a feeling of crispness)
Sparkling wines	Champagne Crémants Prosecco		Fruity and floral aromas (rosés) Pastry aromas	Strong presence of acidity (crispness), sweetness (for the demi-secs and sweet wines)

AGING WINE

Most of the wines we have listed in this book can be uncorked as soon as you have bought them. The only exceptions are the powerful, well-structured reds, which are rich in tannins. The tannins help preserve the wine well, but can impart a hardness to young wines. Light, fruity red wines that have a low tannin content are pleasant to drink as soon as they are purchased but their quality deteriorates relatively quickly. That's why they should be opened within three years. The same is true of almost all the crisp, fruity whites and of numerous sparkling wines. Most rosé wines should be drunk within the year. However, many wines that will go down well as soon as you have purchased them are potentially worth keeping as they improve over several years (see table below).

Type of wine	May be drunk	Aging potential
Red wines: light and fruity	Upon purchase	2 to 3 years
Red wines: fleshy and fruity	Store for at least 3 years, or 5 to 10 years, depending on the appellation and vintage	5 to 10 years
Red wines: powerful and balanced	Store for at least 3 years, or 5 to 10 years, depending on the appellation and vintage	10 years and more 20 years and more for grand crus
Red wines: ripe and spicy	Upon purchase Store for 2 to 3 years, depending on the appellation and vintage	5 years 20 years for some appellations and vintages
Red wines: sweet	Upon purchase (for sweet reds, tawny style) Store for 5 years (for vintage styles)	20 years (tawny style) 50 years (vintage style)
Rosé wines	Upon purchase	1 year 3 years for certain rosés (Tavel, Bandol)
White wines: crisp and fruity	Upon purchase	3 to 5 years (for the majority) 10 years (certain Rieslings)
White wines: full and round	Upon purchase Store for 2 to 3 years, depending on the appellation and the vintage	5 to 10 years 15 years for Burgundy grand crus
White wines: sweet	Upon purchase for light sweet wines	5 years for light sweet wines 30 years and more for liquoroux such as sauternes and selection de grains noble
Sparkling wines	Upon purchase	5 years 10 years and more for vintage Champagnes

SERVING WINE

To enjoy your wine to the fullest, it should be uncorked carefully, and served and maintained at the right temperature, allowing all its aromas and the balance of flavors to be expressed. If you're serving several wines, plan the order in which you'll pour them. And don't forget to provide a jug of water!

UNCORKING THE BOTTLE: WINE OPENERS

Twist and pull corkscrew

Hard to use— these corkscrews pierce the cork

Winged butterfly or double lever corkscrew

May not look professional, but practical

Waiter's corkscrew

The tool of professionals, with a small lever that, when pressed on the neck of the bottle, allows you to draw the cork up.

Screw pull®

Easy and effective.

Essentials to keep in mind

- Cut the capsule below the ring of the bottleneck
- Don't pierce the cork by screwing in the coil too far: bits of cork will fall into the bottle
- To open a Champagne bottle: Remove the capsule and untwist the muzzle (the twisted wire), holding the cork down with one hand. Holding the bottle by the base, pivot the bottle. Don't allow the cork to spring out

CHOOSING THE RIGHT GLASS

The tulip-shaped glass

This stemmed glass narrows towards the rim, concentrating the fragrances. It contains between 12 and 15 fl. oz. (35 and 45 ml).

The Champagne flute

A flute is preferable to a coupe (or Champagne saucer), which allows the bubbles to escape rapidly. It should be neither too narrow nor too straight.

SERVING WINE AT THE CORRECT TEMPERATURE

Type of wine	Ideal temperature range
Red wines: light and fruity	57–61°F (14–16°C)
Red wines: fleshy and fruity	59–63°F (15–17°C)
Red wines: powerful and balanced	Bordeaux: 61–64°F (16–18°C) Burgundy: 59–61°F (15–16°C)
Red wines: ripe and spicy	57–61°F (14–16°C)
Red wines: sweet	59–61°F (15–16°C)
Rosé wines	46–50°F (8–10°C)
Whites wines: crisp and fruity	46–50°F (8–10°C)
Whites wines: full and round	50–54/57°F (10–12/14°C)
White wines: sweet	46–48°F (8–9°C)
Sparkling wines	46–48°F (8–9°C)

MORE THAN ONE WINE TO SERVE? GO CRESCENDO

White wines: Before the reds.

Wines that should be drunk young: Before aged wines.

Wines aged in vats: Before barrel-aged wines.

Lighter wines: Before those with a higher alcohol content

Dry wines: Before sweet wines

Wines that should be served chilled: Before wines at room temperature.

But you may not always be able to respect this order. For example, if you're serving cheese, you'll want a fruity, simple wine, red or even a dry white (to pair with goat cheese). The red meat you might be serving before the cheese pairs with red wines that have more or less backbone.

Solutions: Drink water between each wine; select a single wine that pairs with the main dish.

Did you know?
- Cold temperatures close the tannins of red wines.
- A temperature that is too chilly prevents the aromas from being expressed.
- A temperature that is too high brings out the alcohol and the heavier aromas.

1, 2, 3, 4...?

WINE ACCESSORIES

We'd love to tell you that the only object that you really need is a good corkscrew (see page 32). But you don't need one if your bottle has a cap or if you're opening bag-in-box wine (see page 15)! The most useful accessories are those that enable you to serve wine at the correct temperature so that you can get the most enjoyment out of it. White wines that are too warm have a heaviness, and red wines that are too chilled become acrid. It's important to aerate wine to allow it to breathe and liberate the aromas–enter the carafe. It is especially useful for powerful, well-structured red wines. A duck-shaped decanter is useful only for wine lovers who age their red wines in their cellars.

Standard Decanter

Aerates the wine whose aromas are liberated more freely; the tannins of young red wines soften

Ice bucket

Refreshes wines. Alternatively: an insulated chiller bag you can keep in your freezer

Duck-Shaped Decanter

With this, you can remove the sediment of powerful, tannic reds.

Wine cooler

Keeps the wine at a constant temperature

Wine bottle cradle

So you can pour cellared red wines without including their sediment or exposing them to air, which can alter them irremediably

Wine thermometer

To be sure to serve the wine at the correct temperature

Drip stop

Prevents stains on the tablecloth

Vacuum pump

Creates a vacuum in an unfinished bottle of wine, preserving the wine for a few days

PAIRINGS AND MISMATCHES

Because of their texture or aromas, there are certain dishes that are hard to pair with wines, but they are few and far between. Other dishes will only pair with certain wine categories.

A FEW GUIDELINES TO KEEP IN MIND

 Green vegetables

Green vegetables "harden" wines, particularly when they are contained in water-based soups. Green vegetables served on their own do not make for thrilling pairings with wine, even if they can content themselves with crisp, fruity whites; light, fruity reds; and dry rosés. However, since vegetables are often served as sides to meat, the pairing is made with the main component of the dish. Asparagus, which have a very pronounced taste, alter the flavor of many wines, with the exception of some crisp, fruity whites, like dry muscats.

 Shellfish and fish

Raw oysters and shellfish, and highly iodized sea fish, do not go well with red wines. Some fans of these foods, though, like them with very dry rosés. You can make your selection among the crisp, fruity white wines. When these ingredients are cooked with cream or butter, the dish pairs well with full, round whites, and when they're cooked with olive oil, rosés work well.

 Red meat

(beef, lamb, duck)

Red meat—whether grilled, roasted, or served with a sauce—does not pair well with white wines. However, it goes wonderfully well with slightly tannic reds, reds that are fleshy and fruity, and any that are strong and balanced.

 White meat

(veal, pork, chicken, turkey)

White meats of all types are very accommodating, pairing well with most wine categories. Since these meats have a delicate taste, the only thing to avoid is putting them face-to-face with strong, well-structured wines and the firmest of the ripe wines.

 Eggs

The texture of eggs lines the palate, and so egg will only tolerate lively wines, which you should select among the crisp, fruity whites; dry rosés; light, fruity reds; and the least tannic of the fleshy, fruity reds.

Spices and condiments

Spices, used in many cuisines around the world, pair with a good number of wines—in particular, ripe, spicy reds as well as rosé wines. However, when spices are liberally used, they tend to flatten out the taste of the most robust crus. And the same is true of condiments, such as garlic, used in excess. Wine has a couple of "enemies," including vinegar and mustard. You can use a few drops of balsamic vinegar, though. In gastronomy, just as in wine tasting, it's excess that spoils everything!

Cheese

Strong-tasting cheeses, like blue cheeses and soft cheeses like camembert, will ruin many wines. Generally speaking, they don't pair at all with low-alcohol and low-acidity wines, and they have little affinity for tannic, well-structured wines (with the exception of sweet reds, like port). On the whole, there is less risk of making a blooper if you select a white wine—dry or sweet—as long as it is sufficiently ample and acidic.

Desserts

Avoid pairing sweet desserts (creamy cakes and Middle Eastern pastries) with dry wines, including Champagne and other sparkling wines—they will come across as aggressive. The exception is demi-sec and sweet sparkling wines, as well as a few rosés. Of course, you can always pair desserts with wines, even with a sweet wine, but it will be heavy and add calories. Dry wines, with or without bubbles, may be paired with fruit.

FOOD AND WINE: CLASSIC PRINCIPLES FOR PAIRING

	Red Wines	White Wines	Rosé Wines	Sparkling Wines
Locavore pairings	Bordeaux and porcini from Bordeaux Beaujolais and Lyon sausages	Riesling from Alsace with sauerkraut and pork	Côte de Provence and ratatouille	Champagne and Chaource cheese
Complementary matching	Rich, unctuous Banyuls (natural sweet wine) and chocolate cake	Fleshy, well-rounded Meursault and white meat with sauce	Fruity, suave Cabernet d'Anjou and dessert with red fruit	Suave Clairette de Die and crepes flavored with orange blossom water
Bring opposites together	Sweet white wine (liquoureux) and salty blue cheese with a bitter taste	Lively Touraine Sauvignon and fatty charcuterie, such as rillettes	Lively Côte de Toul with quiche	Champagne Brut and fish dish with sauce

WINE AND DINE:
OUR SECRETS FOR SUCCESSFUL PAIRINGS

The art of pairing wine and food is not all that complicated. Each category of wines has an affinity for particular types of recipes, and there are certain dishes with which some wine categories should not be served. If you're not an experienced sommelier, it's best to avoid the following pairings: white wine with red meat; red wine with iodine-rich dishes like shellfish and raw fish; and brut sparkling wines with desserts. Here's a quick recap of the principles you should keep in mind (see pictograms key, pg. 218).

	Red wines: light and fruity	Red wines: fleshy and fruity	Red wines: powerful, balanced	Red wines: ripe and spicy	Red wines: sweet	Rosés
Nibbles and starters						
Fish and other seafood						
Mushrooms						
Cuisines from around the world						
Meat and poultry						
Cheese						
Desserts						

	White wines: crisp and fruity	White wines: full and round	White wines: sweet	Sparkling wines: dry	Sparkling wines: semi-dry & sweet
Nibbles and starters					
Fish and other seafood					
Mushrooms					
Cuisines of the world					
Fish and other seafood					
Meat and poultry					
Cheese					
Desserts					

The main categories of dishes

- aperitif
- barbecue
- grilled beef
- duck
- mushrooms
- charcuterie
- shellfish
- scallops
- custardy desserts
- crustaceans (small)

- foie gras
- soft cheese
- washed rind cheese
- pressed cheese
- blue cheese
- goat milk cheese
- feathered game
- furred game
- oysters

- sushi, raw fish
- fish with sauce
- grilled fish
- quiches and savory tarts
- truffles
- white meat
- red meat with sauce
- roasted red meat
- poultry

FINDING THE WINE THAT SUITS YOU

To find out which wine you're probably going to like, answer the questions below. The wines will pair with your favorite dishes and be ideal for whenever you just feel like opening a bottle.

YOU LIKE TO UNCORK A BOTTLE FOR:

A picnic or barbecue
- Beaujolais ●●●
- Bergerac ●●●
- Haut-Poitou ●●●
- Picpoul de Pinet ●
- Rosé d'Anjou ●
- Ventoux ●●●

A potluck meal
- Anjou ●●
- Costières de Nîmes ●●●
- Côtes du Roussillon ●●●
- Coteaux Varois en Provence ●●●
- Fronton ●●
- Mâcon-Villages ●

A buffet
- Champagne ●●
- Crémants ●●
- Prosecco ●●
- Pouilly-Fumé ●
- Côtes du Rhône ●●●
- Médoc ●

A refined, tête-à-tête dinner
- Alsace *vendanges tardives* ●
- Champagne ●●
- Condrieu ●
- Chambolle-Musigny ●
- Corton-Charlemagne ●
- Margaux ●

WHEN YOU BUY A BOTTLE

You uncork it immediately
- Bordeaux ●●●
- Champagne ●●
- Côtes de Provence ●●●
- Mâcon ●●
- Touraine Sauvignon ●
- Ventoux ●●●

You put it in your new cellar: you're starting a wine collection
- Alsace Riesling ●
- Barolo ●
- Bandol ●
- Chablis Grand Cru ●
- Cornas ●
- Hermitage ●●
- Nuits-Saint-Georges ●
- Pessac-Léognan ●●
- Vintage Port ●
- Quarts de Chaume ●
- Saint-Estèphe ●
- Sauternes ●
- Ribera del Duero ●
- Vin Jaune ●

PAIRING WINE WITH YOUR FAVORITE FOODS

Oysters	Chablis ● Champagne (brut, blanc de blancs) ● Alsace Sylvaner ●	Entre-Deux-Mers ● Muscadet Sèvre et Maine ● Picpoul de Pinet ●	
Sushi and raw fish	Alsace Riesling ● White Bordeaux ● Jurançon sec ●	Muscadet Sèvre et Maine ● Pouilly-Fumé ● Sancerre ●	
Quiches and other savory tarts	Alsace Pinot Blanc ● Burgundy ● ● ● Côtes de Toul ● ● ●	Touraine Sauvignon ● Coteaux du Vendômois ● ● Savoie ● ● ●	
Rib-eye steak	Cahors ● Chinon ● Côte-Rôtie ●	Minervois ● Pommard ● Pauillac ●	
Red meat dishes with sauce	Bandol ● Barolo ● Burgundy ● Corbières ● Côtes du Rhône ●	Côtes du Roussillon ● Juliénas ● Madiran ● Mâcon ● Savoie Mondeuse ●	
Roast chicken	Alsace Pinot Gris ● Bordeaux ● ● Chiroubles ●	Côtes de Duras ● ● Saint-Véran ● Saumur-Champigny ●	
Scallops	Champagne ● Vouvray sec and sparkling ● Pessac-Léognan ●	Savennières ● Pouilly-Fuissé ● Saint-Joseph ●	
Grilled fish	Alsace Riesling ● Bandol ● ● Bordeaux ● Cassis ● ● Jurançon ●	Touraine Sauvignon ● Pinot Grigio ● Rias Baixas ● Rueda ● Vinho Verde ●	
Chinese cuisine	Alsace Gewürztraminer ● Cabernet d'Anjou ● Côtes de Provence ●	Côtes du Roussillon ● Tavel ● Sauternes ●	
Mediterranean cuisine	Collioure ● ● ● Corse ● ● ● Costières de Nîmes ● ● ●	Coteaux d'Aix-en-Provence ● ● ● Grignan-les-Adhémar ● ● Languedoc ● ● ●	
Chocolate cake	Alsace sélection de grains nobles ● Champagne ● Floc de Gascogne ● ● Pineau des Charentes ● ●	Vin de Paille (arbois, côtes-du-jura) ● Vins doux Naturels Grenat or Tuilés ●	

YOUR FAVORITE PLACE TO UNCORK A BOTTLE

A candlelit dinner	Chablis grand cru ● Champagne ● ● Hermitage ● ●	Meursault ● Saint-julien ● Volnay ●
An outdoor party	Bardolino ● ● Crémants ● ● Côtes de Provence ● ● ●	Fronton ● ● Muscadet Sèvre et Maine ● Quincy ●
A bistro	Brouilly ● Corbières ● Côtes du Rhône Villages ●	Entre-Deux-Mers ● Sancerre ● ● ● Saumur-Champigny ●
Your kitchen	Coteaux Bourguignons ● ● ● Côtes de Duras ● ● ● Crémant ● ●	Haut-Poitou ● ● ● Saumur ● ● Valpolicella ●

YOUR MAXIMUM PRICE

Under $10	Alsace Pinot Blanc ● Anjou ● ● Beaujolais ● ● ● Bergerac ● ● ●	Côtes de Bourg ● Côtes du Rhône ● ● ● Côtes du Roussillon ● ● ● Crémant ● ● Muscadet Sèvre et Maine ●
Under $20	Bourgogne-hautes-côtes ● ● Cahors ● Champagne (RM) ● ● Chinon ● ● ●	Fronsac ● Moulin-à-Vent ● Médoc ● Sancerre ● ● ●
Under $35	Alsace *vendanges tardives* ● Chablis Premier Cru ● Margaux (non-classified) ● Mercurey Premier Cru ● ●	Lalande-de-Pomerol ● Pommard (Village) ● Saint-Émilion Grand Cru ● Saint-Joseph ●
Love knows no limits	Clos-de-vougeot ● Côte-Rôtie ● Champagnes (prestige) ● ● Pauillac Premier cru classé ●	Pomerol (well-known) ● Sauternes Premier cru supérieur ● Porto Vintage ●

YOU GO FOR

Tried and trusted traditional wines	Cahors ● Châteauneuf-du-Pape ● Médoc ●	Pommard ● ● ● Sancerre ● ● ● Vin Jaune (Jura) ●
Taking the road less traveled	Carmenère (Chile) ● Douro ● Pinot Noir (New Zealand) ●	Priorat ● Sauvignon (Marlborough) ● ● Sherry Fino ●

RED WINES: LIGHT AND FRUITY

Anjou
supple and expressive

ORIGIN: FRANCE
Loire Valley (Anjou and Saumur)

VARIETALS   **COLOR**

 cabernet franc

AROMAS

 raspberry   red currants   blackcurrant

blackberry   undergrowth

MOUTHFEEL

Tannins Firmness

1				5					10

Alcohol Heat

1				5					10

Acidity Crispness

1				5					10

SERVE AT 57-61°F **COST** $

BEST TIME TO DRINK

1 year				5 years					10 years

FOOD PAIRINGS

 white meat   poultry

 grilled red meat   red meat with sauce

YOU MIGHT ALSO LIKE

Anjou Villages, Saumur, Saumur-Champigny, Saint-Nicolas-de-Bourgueil, Haut-Poitou, Coteaux du Quercy

---

Bardolino
light and crisp

ORIGIN: ITALY
Veneto

VARIETALS   **COLOR**

 corvina

AROMAS

cherry   raspberry   spices

MOUTHFEEL

Tannins Firmness

1				5					10

Alcohol Heat

1				5					10

Acidity Crispness

1				5					10

SERVE AT 57-61°F **COST** $$

BEST TIME TO DRINK

1 year				5 years					10 years

FOOD PAIRINGS

 charcuterie   grilled red meat

pressed cheese   white meat

YOU MIGHT ALSO LIKE

Valpolicella, Dôle, Beaujolais, Touraine Gamay, Burgundy

Also available in:
 white

44

Also available in:
 rosé

Beaujolais and Beaujolais-Villages
elegant and refined

ORIGIN: FRANCE
Beaujolais

VARIETALS

 gamay

COLOR

AROMAS

 raspberry | blackcurrant | red currants

MOUTHFEEL

Tannins Firmness

1	5	10

Alcohol Heat

1	5	10

Acidity Crispness

1	5	10

SERVE AT 54-57°F **COST** $

BEST TIME TO DRINK

1 year	5 years	10 years

FOOD PAIRINGS

 charcuterie | grilled red meat

 white meat | soft cheese

YOU MIGHT ALSO LIKE

Chiroubles, Fleurie, Brouilly, Touraine Gamay, Anjou Gamay, Dôle, Coteaux du Lyonnais

Brouilly
brackish and refined

ORIGIN: FRANCE
Beaujolais

VARIETALS

gamay

COLOR

AROMAS

strawberry | raspberry | peony

MOUTHFEEL

Tannins Firmness

1	5	10

Alcohol Heat

1	5	10

Acidity Crispness

1	5	10

SERVE AT 57-61°F **COST** $

BEST TIME TO DRINK

1 year	5 years	10 years

FOOD PAIRINGS

white meat | poultry

 red meat with sauce | charcuterie

 soft cheese

YOU MIGHT ALSO LIKE

Chiroubles, Saint-Amour, Fleurie, Beaujolais-Villages, Mâcon, Coteaux du Lyonnais, Touraine Gamay

Also available in:
● white
● rosé

Dolcetto d'Alba
crisp and firm

ORIGIN: ITALY
Piedmont

VARIETALS **COLOR**
 dolcetto

AROMAS
blackcurrant blueberry violet
orange zest tea

MOUTHFEEL
Tannins Firmness
1   5   10

Alcohol Heat
1   5   10

Acidity Crispness
1   5   10

SERVE AT 57-59°F **COST** $ to $$$

BEST TIME TO DRINK
1 year   5 years   10 years

FOOD PAIRINGS
 grilled red meat poultry
 feathered game barbecue

YOU MIGHT ALSO LIKE
Mondeuse (Savoie), Chianti, Valpolicella, Etna Rosso

Dôle
fresh and lively

ORIGIN: SWITZERLAND
Valais

VARIETALS **COLOR**
 pinot noir   gamay

AROMAS
cherry strawberry raspberry
violet blueberry

MOUTHFEEL
Tannins Firmness
1   5   10

Alcohol Heat
1   5   10

Acidity Crispness
1   5   10

SERVE AT 57-59°F **COST** $$

BEST TIME TO DRINK
1 year   5 years   10 years

FOOD PAIRINGS
 charcuterie   grilled red meat
 pressed cheese   white meat

YOU MIGHT ALSO LIKE
Bourgogne Passetoutgrain, Coteaux Bourguignons,
Touraine Gamay

Also available in:
 rosé

Pinot Noir (Anderson Valley)
fresh and fruity

ORIGIN: UNITED STATES
North Coast of California
Mendocino County

VARIETALS   **COLOR**
pinot noir

AROMAS
- cherry
- raspberry
- red plum
- cinnamon
- violet
- toast

MOUTHFEEL

Tannins Firmness

1	5	10

Alcohol Heat

1	5	10

Acidity Crispness

1	5	10

SERVE AT 57-61°F   **COST** $$$ to $$$$

BEST TIME TO DRINK

1 year	5 years	10 years

FOOD PAIRINGS
- furred game
- white meat
- grilled red meat
- poultry

YOU MIGHT ALSO LIKE
Pinot Noir (Marlborough), Pinot Noir (Walker Bay, South Africa), Pinot Noir (Oregon), Pinot Noir (Yarra Valley)

Also available in:
- rosé

Pinot Noir (Los Carneros)
fresh and ethereal

ORIGIN: UNITED STATES
North Coast of California
Napa Valley & Sonoma

VARIETALS   **COLOR**
pinot noir

AROMAS
- cherry
- raspberry
- smoked
- violet
- cinnamon

MOUTHFEEL

Tannins Firmness

1	5	10

Alcohol Heat

1	5	10

Acidity Crispness

1	5	10

SERVE AT 57-59°F   **COST** $$ to $$$

BEST TIME TO DRINK

1 year	5 years	10 years

FOOD PAIRINGS
- white meat
- grilled red meat
- feathered game
- roasted red meat

YOU MIGHT ALSO LIKE
Pinot Noir (Marlborough), Pinot Noir (Walker Bay, South Africa), Pinot Noir (Oregon), Pinot Noir (Yarra Valley)

Also available in:
- rosé

Pinot Noir (Russian River Valley)
crisp and elegant

ORIGIN: UNITED STATES
North Coast of California
Sonoma County

VARIETALS **COLOR**
 pinot noir

AROMAS
 cherry   raspberry   smoked

leather   cinnamon

MOUTHFEEL
Tannins Firmness

1	5	10

Alcohol Heat

1	5	10

Acidity Crispness

1	5	10

SERVE AT 57-61°F **COST** $$ to $$$$

BEST TIME TO DRINK

1 year	5 years	10 years

FOOD PAIRINGS
 grilled red meat   roasted red meat

 feathered game   white meat

YOU MIGHT ALSO LIKE
Pinot Noir (Marlborough), Pinot Noir (Walker Bay, South Africa), Pinot Noir (Oregon), Pinot Noir (Yarra Valley)

Valpolicella
fruity and fresh

ORIGIN: ITALY
Veneto

VARIETALS **COLOR**
 corvina

AROMAS
cherry   blackberry   prune

leather

MOUTHFEEL
Tannins Firmness

1	5	10

Alcohol Heat

1	5	10

Acidity Crispness

1	5	10

SERVE AT 57-61°F **COST** $$

BEST TIME TO DRINK

1 year	5 years	10 years

FOOD PAIRINGS
 charcuterie   grilled red meat

 pressed cheese   white meat

YOU MIGHT ALSO LIKE
Bardolino, Dôle, Beaujolais, Dolcetto d'Alba, Touraine, Red Burgundy

---

Also available in:
rosé

RED WINES: FLESHY AND FRUITY

Bordeaux Blend (Central Valley)
smooth and fruity

ORIGIN: CHILE
Central Valley

VARIETALS
COLOR

 cabernet sauvignon merlot Carménère

AROMAS
- black cherry
- blackberry
- blackcurrant
- red fruit jam
- undergrowth
- toast
- mint
- tobacco

MOUTHFEEL

Tannins Firmness

| 1 | | | | 5 | | | | | 10 |

Alcohol Heat

| 1 | | | | 5 | | | | | 10 |

Acidity Crispness

| 1 | | | | 5 | | | | | 10 |

SERVE AT 59–61°F **COST** $ to $$

BEST TIME TO DRINK

| 1 year | | | | 5 years | | | | | 10 years |

FOOD PAIRINGS
  grilled red meat   roasted red meat
 duck   red meat with sauce

YOU MIGHT ALSO LIKE
Médoc, Méritage (California), Bordeaux-style blends (Stellenbosch), Bordeaux-style blends (Hawke's Bay)

Barbera and blends (California)
lively and fleshy

ORIGIN: UNITED STATES
California

VARIETALS
COLOR

 barbera

AROMAS
- cherry
- raspberry
- spices
- undergrowth
- toast

MOUTHFEEL

Tannins Firmness

| 1 | | | | 5 | | | | | 10 |

Alcohol Heat

| 1 | | | | 5 | | | | | 10 |

Acidity Crispness

| 1 | | | | 5 | | | | | 10 |

SERVE AT 57–61°F **COST** $ to $$$

BEST TIME TO DRINK

| 1 year | | | | 5 years | | | | | 10 years |

FOOD PAIRINGS
 charcuterie   barbecue
 grilled red meat   white meat

YOU MIGHT ALSO LIKE
Barbera d'Alba, Barbera d'Asti, Crus of Beaujolais

Also available in:
○ rosé

Barbera d'Alba and Barbera d'Asti
supple and fruity

ORIGIN: ITALY
Piedmont

VARIETALS

 barbera

COLOR

AROMAS

cherry	raspberry	black pepper
red fruit jam	vanilla	toast

MOUTHFEEL

Tannins Firmness
1   5   10

Alcohol Heat
1   5   10

Acidity Crispness
1   5   10

SERVE AT 61-64°F **COST** $$

BEST TIME TO DRINK
1 year   5 years   10 years

FOOD PAIRINGS

charcuterie	grilled red meat
white meat	poultry
duck	

YOU MIGHT ALSO LIKE
Côtes du Rhône, Pinotage (South Africa),
Languedoc-Roussillon, Pinot Noir (Chile)

Bergerac
dense and aromatic

ORIGIN: FRANCE
Southwest

VARIETALS

 merlot   cabernet franc

COLOR

cabernet sauvignon

AROMAS

blackcurrant	blackberry	cherry
vanilla	toast	undergrowth

MOUTHFEEL

Tannins Firmness
1   5   10

Alcohol Heat
1   5   10

Acidity Crispness
1   5   10

SERVE AT 57-61°F **COST** $

BEST TIME TO DRINK
1 year   5 years   10 years

FOOD PAIRINGS

white meat	poultry
grilled red meat	roasted red meat
feathered game	duck

YOU MIGHT ALSO LIKE
Bordeaux, Buzet, Côtes de Duras, Côtes du Marmandais,
Gaillac, Cabardès, Malepère

Also available in:
white and rosé

Bierzo
elegant and quaffable

ORIGIN: SPAIN
Galicia

VARIETALS
 mencia

COLOR

AROMAS

blackberry — cherry — licorice

thyme — green herbs — toast

black pepper

MOUTHFEEL
Tannins Firmness

1	5	10

Alcohol Heat

1	5	10

Acidity Crispness

1	5	10

SERVE AT 57-61°F   COST $ to $$$$

BEST TIME TO DRINK

1 year	5 years	10 years

FOOD PAIRINGS
grilled red meat — poultry

roasted red meat — feathered game

YOU MIGHT ALSO LIKE
Saumur-Champigny, Red Chinon, Chianti, Buzet

Also available in:

● white
● rosé

Blaye and Blaye Côtes de Bordeaux
robust and balanced

ORIGIN: FRANCE
Bordeaux (Côtes de Bourg, Côtes de Blaye & Premières Côtes de Blaye)

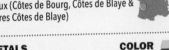

VARIETALS
merlot — cabernet franc — cabernet sauvignon

malbec

COLOR

AROMAS
blackcurrant — blackberry — prune

vanilla — cacao

MOUTHFEEL
Tannins Firmness

1	5	10

Alcohol Heat

1	5	10

Acidity Crispness

1	5	10

SERVE AT 61-64°F   COST $$

BEST TIME TO DRINK

1 year	5 years	10 years

FOOD PAIRINGS
white meat — poultry

grilled red meat — roasted red meat

feathered game — duck

YOU MIGHT ALSO LIKE
Côtes de Bourg, Castillon, Francs Côtes de Bordeaux, Cadillac Côtes de Bordeaux, Bordeaux Supérieur, Cahors, Saint-Mont

Bonarda
supple and fruity

ORIGIN: ARGENTINA
Mendoza

VARIETALS
 bonarda

COLOR

AROMAS
strawberry raspberry mint

clove wood cherry

spices

MOUTHFEEL
Tannins Firmness

1				5					10

Alcohol Heat

1				5					10

Acidity Crispness

1				5					10

SERVE AT 57–59°F **COST** $ to $$

BEST TIME TO DRINK

1 year				5 years				10 years

FOOD PAIRINGS
 charcuterie   grilled red meat

poultry   pressed cheese

duck   barbecue

YOU MIGHT ALSO LIKE
Barbera d'Alba, Red Chinon, Burgundy Pinot Noir, Pinotage

Bordeaux
balanced and approachable

ORIGIN: FRANCE
Bordeaux (regional appellations)

VARIETALS
merlot cabernet franc   **COLOR** cabernet sauvignon

AROMAS
blackcurrant blackberry prune

violet vanilla

MOUTHFEEL
Tannins Firmness

1				5					10

Alcohol Heat

1				5					10

Acidity Crispness

1				5					10

SERVE AT 61–63°F **COST** $

BEST TIME TO DRINK

1 year				5 years				10 years

FOOD PAIRINGS
 charcuterie   white meat

poultry   grilled red meat

roasted red meat

YOU MIGHT ALSO LIKE
Bordeaux Supérieur, Graves de Vayres, Bergerac, Côtes de Duras, Côtes du Marmandais

Also available in:
● white
● rosé and Clairet

53

Bordeaux Supérieur
balanced and round

ORIGIN: FRANCE
Bordeaux (regional appellations)

VARIETALS

 merlot   cabernet franc   **COLOR** cabernet sauvignon

AROMAS

 blackcurrant   blackberry   prune

vanilla   coffee   cacao

MOUTHFEEL

Tannins Firmness

| 1 | | | 5 | | | | 10 |

Alcohol Heat

| 1 | | | 5 | | | | 10 |

Acidity Crispness

| 1 | | | 5 | | | | 10 |

SERVE AT 61-64°F   COST $

BEST TIME TO DRINK

| 1 year | 5 years | 10 years |

FOOD PAIRINGS

 white meat   poultry

 grilled red meat   roasted red meat

duck   mushrooms

YOU MIGHT ALSO LIKE
Saint-Émilion, Côtes de Bourg, Castillon, Francs Côtes de Bordeaux, Cadillac Côtes de Bordeaux, Côtes de Bergerac

---

Bourgogne Côte Chalonnaise
round and firm

ORIGIN: FRANCE
Burgundy (Côte Chalonnaise)

VARIETALS

 pinot noir   **COLOR**

AROMAS

 raspberry   blackcurrant   red currants

cherry   undergrowth

MOUTHFEEL

Tannins Firmness

| 1 | | | 5 | | | | 10 |

Alcohol Heat

| 1 | | | 5 | | | | 10 |

Acidity Crispness

| 1 | | | 5 | | | | 10 |

SERVE AT 57-61°F   COST $

BEST TIME TO DRINK

| 1 year | 5 years | 10 years |

FOOD PAIRINGS

grilled red meat   roasted red meat

red meat with sauce   duck

soft cheese   washed rind cheese

YOU MIGHT ALSO LIKE
Mercurey, Givry, Santenay, Maranges, Pommard

Also available in:
- white
- rosé

Bourgogne Hautes Côtes de Beaune and Côtes de Nuits
dense and full-bodied

ORIGIN: FRANCE
Burgundy (Côte de Nuits vineyards)

VARIETALS   COLOR

 pinot noir

AROMAS

 cherry   raspberry   black pepper

licorice   undergrowth

MOUTHFEEL

Tannins Firmness
1	5	10

Alcohol Heat
1	5	10

Acidity Crispness
1	5	10

SERVE AT 59-61°F **COST** $$

BEST TIME TO DRINK
1 year	5 years	10 years

FOOD PAIRINGS

 grilled red meat   roasted red meat

red meat with sauce   duck

poultry   washed rind cheese

YOU MIGHT ALSO LIKE
Red Burgundy, Beaune, Savigny-lès-Beaune, Chorey-lès-Beaune, Irancy

Also available in:
● white

55

Bourgueil and Saint-Nicolas-de-Bourgueil
fresh and decadent

ORIGIN: FRANCE
Loire Valley (Touraine)

VARIETALS   COLOR

 cabernet franc

AROMAS

 cherry   strawberry   blackcurrant

raspberry   green bell pepper

MOUTHFEEL

Tannins Firmness
1	5	10

Alcohol Heat
1	5	10

Acidity Crispness
1	5	10

SERVE AT 57-61°F **COST** $

BEST TIME TO DRINK
1 year	5 years	10 years

FOOD PAIRINGS

 charcuterie   white meat

poultry   roasted red meat

grilled red meat   pressed cheese

YOU MIGHT ALSO LIKE
Chinon, Saumur-Champigny, Anjou Villages, Anjou Villages Brissac, Touraine Cabernet, Coteaux du Quercy

Also available in:
● rosé

Burgenland Red
supple and spicy

ORIGIN: AUSTRIA
Burgenland

VARIETALS

 blaüfrankisch zweigelt saint-laurent

COLOR

AROMAS

 raspberry   cherry   smoked

wood   licorice   blackcurrant

MOUTHFEEL

Tannins Firmness

1				5					10

Alcohol Heat

1				5					10

Acidity Crispness

1				5					10

SERVE AT 59–63°F   **COST** $ to $$$

BEST TIME TO DRINK

1 year				5 years					10 years

FOOD PAIRINGS

grilled red meat   poultry

feathered game

YOU MIGHT ALSO LIKE
Saumur-Champigny, Bierzo, Pinot Noir (Baden), Chinon

Cabernet Sauvignon (California)
supple and ripe

ORIGIN: UNITED STATES
California

VARIETALS

cabernet
sauvignon

COLOR

AROMAS

black
cherry   black fruit
jam   mint

toast   undergrowth   smoked

MOUTHFEEL

Tannins Firmness

1				5					10

Alcohol Heat

1				5					10

Acidity Crispness

1				5					10

SERVE AT 59–63°F   **COST** $ to $$

BEST TIME TO DRINK

1 year				5 years					10 years

FOOD PAIRINGS

roasted red meat   grilled red meat

duck   roasted red meat

YOU MIGHT ALSO LIKE
Cabernet Sauvignon (Chile), Cabernet Sauvignon
(South Africa), Cabernet Sauvignon (Australia),
Cabernet Sauvignon (Argentina)

Also available in:
rosé

Also available in:
rosé

Carménère (Chile)
fleshy and full-bodied

ORIGIN: CHILE
Chile

VARIETALS
 Carménère

COLOR

AROMAS
 blackberry black pepper red bell pepper

 vanilla toast

MOUTHFEEL

Tannins Firmness

1				5					10

Alcohol Heat

1				5					10

Acidity Crispness

1				5					10

SERVE AT 61-64°F **COST** $$

BEST TIME TO DRINK

1 year			5 years						10 years

FOOD PAIRINGS

 duck   poultry

grilled red meat   roasted red meat

YOU MIGHT ALSO LIKE
Merlot (Chile), Listrac-Médoc, Médoc, Moulis-en-Médoc

Castel del Monte
smooth and spicy

ORIGIN: ITALY
Apulia

VARIETALS
aglianico montepul-ciano uva di Troia

COLOR

AROMAS
 cherry red plum red currants

black pepper leather smoked

MOUTHFEEL

Tannins Firmness

1				5					10

Alcohol Heat

1				5					10

Acidity Crispness

1				5					10

SERVE AT 61-63°F **COST** $ to $$

BEST TIME TO DRINK

1 year			5 years						10 years

FOOD PAIRINGS

grilled red meat   poultry

barbecue   white meat

YOU MIGHT ALSO LIKE
Languedoc-Roussillon, Côtes du Rhône, Côtes du Roussillon, Shiraz-Cabernet Sauvignon (Australia), Zinfandel (California)

Also available in:
● rosé

Also available in:
● white
● rosé

Chianti
supple and fruity

ORIGIN: ITALY
Tuscany

....

VARIETALS   **COLOR**

 sangiovese

AROMAS

 cherry   raspberry   strawberry

green herbs   tea   wood

....

MOUTHFEEL
Tannins Firmness

1	5	10

Alcohol Heat

1	5	10

Acidity Crispness

1	5	10

....

SERVE AT 59-61°F   **COST** $ to $$

BEST TIME TO DRINK

1 year	5 years	10 years

....

FOOD PAIRINGS

 grilled red meat   poultry

 barbecue   Mediterranean cuisine

....

YOU MIGHT ALSO LIKE

Bourgueil, Montepulciano d'Abbruzzo, Rosso di Montalcino, Rosso de Montepulciano, Carmignano

---

Chianti Classico
firm and fruity

ORIGIN: ITALY
Tuscany

....

VARIETALS   **COLOR**

 sangiovese

AROMAS

cherry   red plum   raspberry

violet   spices   vanilla

....

MOUTHFEEL
Tannins Firmness

1	5	10

Alcohol Heat

1	5	10

Acidity Crispness

1	5	10

....

SERVE AT 59-61°F   **COST** $$ to $$$$

BEST TIME TO DRINK

1 year	10 years	20 years

....

FOOD PAIRINGS

 roasted red meat   duck

 feathered game   pressed cheese

 white meat

....

YOU MIGHT ALSO LIKE

Brunello di Montalcino, vino nobile di Montepulciano, Chianti Rufina, Cahors, Savoie Arbin Mondeuse

Chinon
dense and fresh

ORIGIN: FRANCE
Loire Valley (Touraine)

VARIETALS

 cabernet franc

COLOR

AROMAS

raspberry · blackcurrant · cherry

prune

MOUTHFEEL

Tannins Firmness

| 1 | | | | 5 | | | | | 10 |

Alcohol Heat

| 1 | | | | 5 | | | | | 10 |

Acidity Crispness

| 1 | | | | 5 | | | | | 10 |

SERVE AT 59-61°F **COST** $ to $$

BEST TIME TO DRINK

| 1 year | | | | 5 years | | | | | 10 years |

FOOD PAIRINGS

white meat   poultry

grilled red meat   roasted red meat

red meat with sauce   feathered game

YOU MIGHT ALSO LIKE

Bourgueil, Saint-Nicolas-de-Bourgueil, Saumur-Champigny, Anjou Villages Brissac

Also available in:
● white
● rosé

Côtes de Bourg
robust and aromatic

ORIGIN: FRANCE
Bordeaux (Côtes de Bourg, Côtes de Blaye & Premières Côtes de Blaye)

VARIETALS

merlot · malbec · cabernet franc

cabernet sauvignon

COLOR

AROMAS

cherry · blackberry · prune

vanilla · cacao

MOUTHFEEL

Tannins Firmness

| 1 | | | | 5 | | | | | 10 |

Alcohol Heat

| 1 | | | | 5 | | | | | 10 |

Acidity Crispness

| 1 | | | | 5 | | | | | 10 |

SERVE AT 61-63°F **COST** $

BEST TIME TO DRINK

| 1 year | | | | 5 years | | | | | 10 years |

FOOD PAIRINGS

charcuterie   roasted red meat

grilled red meat   feathered game

pressed cheese

YOU MIGHT ALSO LIKE

Blaye, Castillon, Francs Côtes de Bordeaux, Cadillac Côtes de Bordeaux, Fronsac, Sainte-Foy-Bordeaux, Bordeaux Supérieur, Pécharmant

Also available in:
● white

Crozes-Hermitage
supple and spicy

ORIGIN: FRANCE
Northern Rhone Valley

VARIETALS

 syrah

COLOR

AROMAS

cherry | licorice | violet
peony | black pepper

MOUTHFEEL

Tannins Firmness
1   5   10

Alcohol Heat
1   5   10

Acidity Crispness
1   5   10

SERVE AT 59-61°F **COST** $$

BEST TIME TO DRINK
1 year   5 years   10 years

FOOD PAIRINGS

 grilled red meat
 red meat with sauce
duck
 feathered game
white meat
Middle Eastern cuisine

YOU MIGHT ALSO LIKE
Saint-Joseph, Côtes du Rhône Villages

Also available in:
 white

60

Dão
fleshy and elegant

ORIGIN: PORTUGAL
Dâo

VARIETALS

 touriga nacional
 alfrocheiro
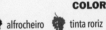 tinta roriz
 jaen

COLOR

AROMAS

blackberry | strawberry | wood
spices | blackcurrant | blueberry
licorice

MOUTHFEEL

Tannins Firmness
1   5   10

Alcohol Heat
1   5   10

Acidity Crispness
1   5   10

SERVE AT 61-63°F **COST** $ to $$$

BEST TIME TO DRINK
1 year   5 years   10 years

FOOD PAIRINGS

 grilled red meat
 poultry
 roasted red meat
 feathered game

YOU MIGHT ALSO LIKE
Côtes du Rhône Villages, Crozes-Hermitage,
Languedoc-Roussillon, Douro, Rioja, Ribera del Duero

Also available in:
 white
rosé

Friuli Grave
supple and fruity

ORIGIN: ITALY
Veneto

VARIETALS **COLOR**

 merlot cabernet sauvignon Carménère

AROMAS

 raspberry  blackcurrant black cherry

undergrowth green bell pepper wood

MOUTHFEEL

Tannins Firmness

| 1 | | | | 5 | | | | | 10 |

Alcohol Heat

| 1 | | | | 5 | | | | | 10 |

Acidity Crispness

| 1 | | | | 5 | | | | | 10 |

SERVE AT 57-61°F **COST** $ to $$

BEST TIME TO DRINK

| 1 year | | | | 5 years | | | | | 10 years |

FOOD PAIRINGS

 grilled red meat poultry

barbecue white meat

YOU MIGHT ALSO LIKE

Merlot (California), Bordeaux, Bordeaux Supérieur,
Blaye Côtes de Bordeaux, Merlot (Chile)

Fronsac
dense and round

ORIGIN: FRANCE
Bordeaux (The Vineyards of Libourne)

VARIETALS **COLOR**

 merlot cabernet franc cabernet sauvignon

AROMAS

 blackberry black cherry blackcurrant

 vanilla coffee

MOUTHFEEL

Tannins Firmness

| 1 | | | | 5 | | | | | 10 |

Alcohol Heat

| 1 | | | | 5 | | | | | 10 |

Acidity Crispness

| 1 | | | | 5 | | | | | 10 |

SERVE AT 61-64°F **COST** $$

BEST TIME TO DRINK

| 1 year | | | | 5 years | | | | | 10 years |

FOOD PAIRINGS

 grilled red meat roasted red meat

 duck feathered game

 mushrooms pressed cheese

YOU MIGHT ALSO LIKE

Castillon, Francs Côtes de Bordeaux, Canon-Fronsac,
Lalande-de-Pomerol, Saint-Émilion, Côtes de Bourg,
Pécharmant, Côtes de Bergerac

Also available in:
 white
rosé

Gaillac
rich and round

ORIGIN: FRANCE
Southwest

VARIETALS **COLOR**

 duras fer-servadou syrah

 cabernet sauvignon cabernet franc

AROMAS

blackcurrant raspberry cherry

prune black pepper

MOUTHFEEL

Tannins Firmness
1　　　5　　　10

Alcohol Heat
1　　　5　　　10

Acidity Crispness
1　　　5　　　10

SERVE AT 61-63°F **COST** $

BEST TIME TO DRINK
1 year　　5 years　　10 years

FOOD PAIRINGS

 white meat　roasted red meat

grilled red meat　duck

pressed cheese

YOU MIGHT ALSO LIKE
Marcillac, Saint-Sardos, Brulhois, Bergerac

Also available in:
● white
● rosé

62

Graves
firm and seductive

ORIGIN: FRANCE
Bordeaux (Graves)

VARIETALS **COLOR**

cabernet sauvignon merlot cabernet franc

AROMAS

 blackcurrant cherry violet

 smoked coffee vanilla

MOUTHFEEL

Tannins Firmness
1　　　5　　　10

Alcohol Heat
1　　　5　　　10

Acidity Crispness
1　　　5　　　10

SERVE AT 61-64°F **COST** $$

BEST TIME TO DRINK
1 year　5 years　10 years

FOOD PAIRINGS

 grilled red meat　 roasted red meat

duck　feathered game

 mushrooms　 pressed cheese

YOU MIGHT ALSO LIKE
Médoc, Haut-Médoc, Passac-Léognan,
Moulis-en-Médoc, Listrac-Médoc

Also available in:
● white

Médoc
robust and round

ORIGIN: FRANCE
Bordeaux (Médoc vineyards)

VARIETALS

COLOR

cabernet sauvignon

merlot

petit verdot

cabernet franc

AROMAS

blackcurrant blackberry vanilla

cacao undergrowth toast

MOUTHFEEL

Tannins Firmness

1	5	10

Alcohol Heat

1	5	10

Acidity Crispness

1	5	10

SERVE AT 61-64°F COST $$

BEST TIME TO DRINK

1 year	5 years	10 years	15 years	20 years

FOOD PAIRINGS

grilled red meat roasted red meat

duck white meat

poultry feathered game

YOU MIGHT ALSO LIKE
Haut-Médoc, Graves, Moulis-en-Médoc, Côtes de Bourg, Bordeaux Supérieur, Pécharmant, Côtes de Bergerac

---

Mercurey
firm and elegant

ORIGIN: FRANCE
Burgundy (Côte Chalonnaise)

VARIETALS

COLOR

pinot noir

AROMAS

cherry raspberry strawberry

blackcurrant undergrowth leather

vanilla

MOUTHFEEL

Tannins Firmness

1	5	10

Alcohol Heat

1	5	10

Acidity Crispness

1	5	10

SERVE AT 59-61°F COST $$

BEST TIME TO DRINK

1 year	5 years	10 years

FOOD PAIRINGS

grilled red meat roasted red meat

red meat with sauce duck

furred game feathered game

YOU MIGHT ALSO LIKE
Pommard, Beaune, Santenay, Chassagne-Montrachet, Givry, barrel-aged Pinot Noir (Alsace)

Also available in:
 white

Merlot (California)
round and fruity

ORIGIN: UNITED STATES
California

VARIETALS **COLOR**
merlot

AROMAS
 red fruit jam   black cherry   blackberry
cacao   toast

MOUTHFEEL
Tannins Firmness

| 1 | | | 5 | | | 10 |

Alcohol Heat

| 1 | | | 5 | | | 10 |

Acidity Crispness

| 1 | | | 5 | | | 10 |

SERVE AT 57–61°F   **COST** $ to $$

BEST TIME TO DRINK

| 1 year | | 5 years | | 10 years |

FOOD PAIRINGS
roasted red meat   grilled red meat
duck   barbecue

YOU MIGHT ALSO LIKE
Merlot (Chile), Merlot (Sicily), Merlot (Veneto), Merlot (Australia)

Merlot (Central Valley)
round and supple

ORIGIN: CHILE
Central Valley

VARIETALS **COLOR**
merlot

AROMAS
black cherry   red plum   red fruit jam
mint   green bell pepper   wood
undergrowth

MOUTHFEEL
Tannins Firmness

| 1 | | | 5 | | | 10 |

Alcohol Heat

| 1 | | | 5 | | | 10 |

Acidity Crispness

| 1 | | | 5 | | | 10 |

SERVE AT 59–61°F   **COST** $ to $$

BEST TIME TO DRINK

| 1 year | | 5 years | | 10 years |

FOOD PAIRINGS
grilled red meat   white meat
barbecue

YOU MIGHT ALSO LIKE
Red Grave del Friuli, IGP Pays d'Oc Merlot, Merlot (California), Bordeaux, Bordeaux Supérieur, Blaye Côtes de Bordeaux, Carménère (Chile)

Also available in:
rosé

Also available in:
rosé

Merlot (Columbia Valley)
intense and fleshy

ORIGIN: UNITED STATES
Washington
Columbia Valley

VARIETALS

merlot

COLOR

AROMAS

 raspberry

red plum

red fruit jam

vanilla

toast

undergrowth

MOUTHFEEL
Tannins Firmness

1	5	10

Alcohol Heat

1	5	10

Acidity Crispness

1	5	10

SERVE AT 59-61°F **COST** $ to $$$

BEST TIME TO DRINK

1 year	5 years	10 years

FOOD PAIRINGS

 roasted red meat

 grilled red meat

 red meat with sauce

 duck

YOU MIGHT ALSO LIKE
Merlot (Chile), Merlot (Sicily), Saint-Émilion, Côtes de Bourg

Also available in:
rosé

Merlot (Napa Valley)
fleshy and opulent

ORIGIN: UNITED STATES
North Coast of California
Napa Valley

VARIETALS

 merlot

COLOR

AROMAS

 black cherry

toast

red plum

smoked

red fruit jam

mint

MOUTHFEEL
Tannins Firmness

1	5	10

Alcohol Heat

1	5	10

Acidity Crispness

1	5	10

SERVE AT 57-61°F **COST** $$$ to $$$$$

BEST TIME TO DRINK

1 year	5 years	10 years

FOOD PAIRINGS

 roasted red meat

 grilled red meat

 truffle

 red meat with sauce

YOU MIGHT ALSO LIKE
Pomerol, Saint-Emilion Grand Cru, Merlot (Colchagua)

Also available in:
rosé

Merlot and Blends (Hawke's Bay)
fleshy and soft

ORIGIN: NEW ZEALAND
North Island

VARIETALS

 merlot cabernet-sauvignon

COLOR

AROMAS

 red plum · cherry · undergrowth

toast · green herbs

MOUTHFEEL

Tannins Firmness
1   5   10

Alcohol Heat
1   5   10

Acidity Crispness
1   5   10

SERVE AT 59-63°F   **COST** $$ to $$$$$

BEST TIME TO DRINK
1 year   5 years   10 years

FOOD PAIRINGS

 grilled red meat   poultry

red meat with sauce   duck

YOU MIGHT ALSO LIKE
Médoc, Méritage (California), Bordeaux-style blends (Stellenbosch), Bordeaux-style blends (Central Valley, Chile)

Also available in:
 rosé

66

Morgon
robust and complex

ORIGIN: FRANCE
Beaujolais

VARIETALS
 gamay

COLOR

AROMAS

cherry · blueberry · blackcurrant

minerality

MOUTHFEEL

Tannins Firmness
1   5   10

Alcohol Heat
1   5   10

Acidity Crispness
1   5   10

SERVE AT 57-61°F   **COST** $

BEST TIME TO DRINK
1 year   5 years   10 yea

FOOD PAIRINGS

 white meat   grilled red meat

 red meat with sauce   furred game

pressed cheese

YOU MIGHT ALSO LIKE
Moulin-à-Vent, Juliénas, Côte de Brouilly, Chénas, Régnié, Fleurie, Beaujolais-Villages, Saint-Amour

Moulin-à-vent
full-bodied and refined

ORIGIN: FRANCE
Beaujolais

VARIETALS
 gamay

COLOR

AROMAS

cherry

strawberry

blueberry

violet

rose

vanilla

MOUTHFEEL
Tannins Firmness

1	5	10

Alcohol Heat

1	5	10

Acidity Crispness

1	5	10

SERVE AT 57–61°F COST $

BEST TIME TO DRINK

1 year	5 years	10 years

FOOD PAIRINGS
 white meat

poultry

grilled red meat

red meat with sauce

furred game

pressed cheese

YOU MIGHT ALSO LIKE
Morgon, Côte de Brouilly, Chénas, Juliénas, Fleurie, Brouilly, Saint-Amour, Régnié, Beaujolais-Villages

---

Nero d'Avola (Sicily)
supple and spicy

ORIGIN: ITALY
Sicily

VARIETALS
 nero d'Avola

COLOR

AROMAS
 black cherry

 licorice

 black fruit jam

smoked

wood

spices

licorice

MOUTHFEEL
Tannins Firmness

1	5	10

Alcohol Heat

1	5	10

Acidity Crispness

1	5	10

SERVE AT 59–61°F COST $ to $$$

BEST TIME TO DRINK

1 year	5 years	10 years

FOOD PAIRINGS
 grilled red meat

 poultry

 red meat with sauce

 Mediterranean cuisine

YOU MIGHT ALSO LIKE
Primitivo di Puglia, Castel del Monte Rosso, Faugères, Ribera del Duero, Côtes du Roussillon

Pinot Noir (Oregon)
well-structured and fragrant

ORIGIN: UNITED STATES
Oregon

VARIETALS
 pinot noir

COLOR

AROMAS

cherry	red plum	raspberry
cinnamon	toast	peony

MOUTHFEEL

Tannins Firmness

1	5	10

Alcohol Heat

1	5	10

Acidity Crispness

1	5	10

SERVE AT 57-61°F **COST** $$$ to $$$$$

BEST TIME TO DRINK

1 year	5 years	10 years

FOOD PAIRINGS

 feathered game
grilled red meat
poultry
duck

YOU MIGHT ALSO LIKE
Pinot Noir (Casablanca), Pommard, Nuits-Saint-Georges, Pinot Noir (Yarra Valley)

Pinot Noir (Baden)
rich and intense

ORIGIN: GERMANY
Baden

VARIETALS
 pinot noir

COLOR

AROMAS

cherry	raspberry	smoked
toast	leather	gibier

MOUTHFEEL

Tannins Firmness

1	5	10

Alcohol Heat

1	5	10

Acidity Crispness

1	5	10

SERVE AT 57-61°F **COST** $$ to $$$

BEST TIME TO DRINK

1 year	5 years	10 years

FOOD PAIRINGS

grilled red meat
feathered game
duck

YOU MIGHT ALSO LIKE
Gevrey-Chambertin, Pinot Noir (Santa Barbara), Pinot Noir (Central Otago)

Also available in:
rosé

Pinot Noir (Casablanca Valley)
fruity and supple

ORIGIN: CHILE
Casablanca Valley

VARIETALS
 pinot noir

COLOR

AROMAS

 raspberry   red plum   cherry

leather   peony   red fruit jam

caramel

MOUTHFEEL
Tannins Firmness

| 1 | 5 | 10 |

Alcohol Heat

| 1 | 5 | 10 |

Acidity Crispness

| 1 | 5 | 10 |

SERVE AT 55-59°F **COST** $ to $$$

BEST TIME TO DRINK

| 1 year | 5 years | 10 years |

FOOD PAIRINGS

 grilled red meat   poultry

white meat   feathered game

 barbecue

YOU MIGHT ALSO LIKE
Pinot Noir (Yarra Valley), Côtes de Nuits Villages, Pinot Noir (Walker Bay, South Africa)

Also available in:
● rosé

Pinot Noir (Central Otago)
powerful and juicy

ORIGIN: NEW ZEALAND
South Island

VARIETALS
pinot noir

COLOR

AROMAS

raspberry   cherry   red fruit jam

toast   red plum

MOUTHFEEL
Tannins Firmness

| 1 | 5 | 10 |

Alcohol Heat

| 1 | 5 | 10 |

Acidity Crispness

| 1 | 5 | 10 |

SERVE AT 59-61°F **COST** $$ to $$$$$$

BEST TIME TO DRINK

| 1 year | 5 years | 10 years |

FOOD PAIRINGS

 grilled red meat   poultry

roasted red meat   feathered game

 barbecue

YOU MIGHT ALSO LIKE
Pommard, Pinot Noir (Yarra Valley), Pinot Noir (Willamette Valley), Pinot Noir (Oregon)

Also available in:
● rosé

Pinot Noir (New Zealand)
crisp and aromatic

ORIGIN: NEW ZEALAND

Marlborough and Central Otago

VARIETALS

COLOR

 pinot noir

AROMAS

 cherry   raspberry   spices

leather   toast   undergrowth

MOUTHFEEL

Tannins Firmness

| 1 | | | | 5 | | | | | 10 |

Alcohol Heat

| 1 | | | | 5 | | | | | 10 |

Acidity Crispness

| 1 | | | | 5 | | | | | 10 |

SERVE AT 59-61°F **COST** $$$

BEST TIME TO DRINK

| 1 year | | | | 5 years | | | | | 10 years |

FOOD PAIRINGS

 charcuterie   white meat

grilled red meat   feathered game

 poultry

YOU MIGHT ALSO LIKE

Côtes de Nuits Villages, Fixin, Pinot Noir (Chile), Pinot Noir (Walker Bay, South Africa)

Also available in:
● rosé

Pinot Noir (Monterey)
supple and fruity

ORIGIN: UNITED STATES

Central Coast of California
Monterey County

VARIETALS

COLOR

 pinot noir

AROMAS

cherry   raspberry   cinnamon

toast   undergrowth   smoked

MOUTHFEEL

Tannins Firmness

| 1 | | | | 5 | | | | | 10 |

Alcohol Heat

| 1 | | | | 5 | | | | | 10 |

Acidity Crispness

| 1 | | | | 5 | | | | | 10 |

SERVE AT 57-61°F **COST** $$ to $$$$

BEST TIME TO DRINK

| 1 year | | | | 5 years | | | | | 10 years |

FOOD PAIRINGS

white meat   grilled red meat

 feathered game   duck

YOU MIGHT ALSO LIKE

Pinot Noir (Marlborough), Pinot Noir (Walker Bay, South Africa), Pinot Noir (Oregon), Pinot Noir (Tasmania)

Also available in:
● rosé

70

Pinot Noir
(Santa Barbara)
complex and expressive

ORIGIN: UNITED STATES
Central Coast of California
Santa Barbara County

VARIETALS **COLOR**

pinot noir

AROMAS

cherry · leather · raspberry

red plum · undergrowth · spices

toast

MOUTHFEEL

Tannins Firmness

1				5					10

Alcohol Heat

1				5					10

Acidity Crispness

1				5					10

SERVE AT 57–61°F **COST** $$$ to $$$$

BEST TIME TO DRINK

1 year				5 years					10 years

FOOD PAIRINGS

grilled red meat · feathered game

white meat · furred game

YOU MIGHT ALSO LIKE

Pinot Noir (Casablanca), Pommard, Nuits-Saint-Georges,
Pinot Noir (Yarra Valley)

Pinot Noir
(Santa Maria Valley)
complex and expressive

ORIGIN: UNITED STATES
Central Coast of California
Santa Barbara County

VARIETALS **COLOR**

pinot noir

AROMAS

cherry · raspberry · leather

toast · smoked · spices

MOUTHFEEL

Tannins Firmness

1				5					10

Alcohol Heat

1				5					10

Acidity Crispness

1				5					10

SERVE AT 57–61°F **COST** $$$ to $$$$$

BEST TIME TO DRINK

1 year				5 years					10 years

FOOD PAIRINGS

poultry · grilled red meat

furred game · feathered game

YOU MIGHT ALSO LIKE

Pinot Noir (Casablanca), Pommard, Nuits-Saint-Georges,
Pinot Noir (Yarra Valley)

Also available in:
 rosé

71

Pinot Noir (Walker Bay)
complex and delicate

ORIGIN: SOUTH AFRICA
Cape South Coast

VARIETALS   **COLOR**
 pinot noir

AROMAS

 cherry   raspberry   cinnamon

wood   peony   game

 undergrowth

MOUTHFEEL

Tannins Firmness
| 1 | | | | 5 | | | | | 10 |

Alcohol Heat
| 1 | | | | 5 | | | | | 10 |

Acidity Crispness
| 1 | | | | 5 | | | | | 10 |

SERVE AT 57–61°F **COST** $$$ to $$$$

BEST TIME TO DRINK
| 1 year | | | 5 years | | | | | 10 years |

FOOD PAIRINGS

 grilled red meat   poultry

 duck

YOU MIGHT ALSO LIKE

Pinot Noir (Casablanca), Côtes de Nuits Villages,
Pinot Noir (Yarra Valley), Volnay

Pinot Noir (Willamette Valley)
complex and intense

ORIGIN: UNITED STATES
Oregon
Willamette Valley

VARIETALS   **COLOR**
 pinot noir

AROMAS

 cherry   raspberry   toast

undergrowth cinnamon   leather

MOUTHFEEL

Tannins Firmness
| 1 | | | | 5 | | | | | 10 |

Alcohol Heat
| 1 | | | | 5 | | | | | 10 |

Acidity Crispness
| 1 | | | | 5 | | | | | 10 |

SERVE AT 57–61°F **COST** $$$ to $$$$$

BEST TIME TO DRINK
| 1 year | | | 10 years | | | | | 20 years |

FOOD PAIRINGS

 white meat   feathered game

 grilled red meat   duck

YOU MIGHT ALSO LIKE

Pinot Noir (Casablanca), Pommard, Nuits-Saint-Georges,
Pinot Noir (Yarra Valley)

72

Also available in:
● rosé

Pinot Noir (Yarra Valley)
fragrant and lively

ORIGIN: AUSTRALIA
Victoria

VARIETALS

 pinot noir

COLOR

AROMAS

 raspberry red plum Morello cherry

blueberry cinnamon wood

clove

MOUTHFEEL

Tannins Firmness

| 1 | | | 5 | | | | 10 |

Alcohol Heat

| 1 | | | 5 | | | | 10 |

Acidity Crispness

| 1 | | | 5 | | | | 10 |

SERVE AT 55-57°F **COST** $$$ to $$$$$

BEST TIME TO DRINK

| 1 year | 5 years | 10 years |

FOOD PAIRINGS

charcuterie grilled red meat

duck white meat

poultry

YOU MIGHT ALSO LIKE
Pinot Noir (Casablanca), Côtes de Nuits Villages,
Pinot Noir (Walker Bay, South Africa)

Pinot Noir (Pfalz)
fruity and delicate

ORIGIN: GERMANY
The Pfalz

VARIETALS

pinot noir

COLOR

AROMAS

cherry raspberry violet

toast clove cinnamon

game

MOUTHFEEL

Tannins Firmness

| 1 | | | 5 | | | | 10 |

Alcohol Heat

| 1 | | | 5 | | | | 10 |

Acidity Crispness

| 1 | | | 5 | | | | 10 |

SERVE AT 57-61°F **COST** $ to $$$

BEST TIME TO DRINK

| 1 year | 5 years | 10 years |

FOOD PAIRINGS

 grilled red meat poultry

white meat   feathered game

YOU MIGHT ALSO LIKE
Pommard, Fixin, Pinot Noir (Marlborough),
Alsace Pinot Noir

Pinotage (South Africa)
fleshy and fruity

ORIGIN: SOUTH AFRICA

VARIETALS
 pinotage

COLOR

AROMAS

 strawberry   raspberry   cherry

red fruit jam   smoked   leather

licorice

MOUTHFEEL

Tannins Firmness

1		5		10

Alcohol Heat

1		5		10

Acidity Crispness

1		5		10

SERVE AT 57-61°F   **COST** $ to $$

BEST TIME TO DRINK

1 year	5 years	10 years

FOOD PAIRINGS

 grilled red meat   roasted red meat

 duck   barbecue

YOU MIGHT ALSO LIKE

Barbera d'Alba, Côtes du Rhône Villages, Pinot Noir (Casablanca), Castel del Monte Rosso

---

Pinotage (Stellenbosch)
stewed and round

ORIGIN: SOUTH AFRICA
Stellenbosch

VARIETALS
 pinotage

COLOR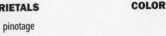

AROMAS

 red fruit jam   raspberry   smoked

  licorice

MOUTHFEEL

Tannins Firmness

1		5		10

Alcohol Heat

1		5		10

Acidity Crispness

1		5		10

SERVE AT 59-61°F   **COST** $$

BEST TIME TO DRINK

1 year	5 years	10 year

FOOD PAIRINGS

 charcuterie   roasted red meat

grilled red meat   furred game

YOU MIGHT ALSO LIKE

Languedoc-Roussillon, Merlot (Chile), Côtes du Rhôn Barbera d'Alba

Also available in:
 rosé

74

Primitivo (Puglia)
smooth and spicy

ORIGIN: ITALY
Puglia

VARIETALS

 primitivo

COLOR

AROMAS

 red fruit jam

blackberry

red plum

licorice

tobacco

scrubland

MOUTHFEEL

Tannins Firmness

1	5	10

Alcohol Heat

1	5	10

Acidity Crispness

1	5	10

SERVE AT 59–63°F **COST** $ to $$$

BEST TIME TO DRINK

1 year	5 years	10 years

FOOD PAIRINGS

grilled red meat

roasted red meat

red meat with sauce

YOU MIGHT ALSO LIKE

Zinfandel (California), Vacqueyras, Yecla, Jumilla

Rioja (Crianza)
supple and fruity

ORIGIN: SPAIN
Rioja

VARIETALS

tempranillo

COLOR

AROMAS

strawberry

raspberry

licorice

vanilla

toast

MOUTHFEEL

Tannins Firmness

1	5	10

Alcohol Heat

1	5	10

Acidity Crispness

1	5	10

SERVE AT 57–61°F **COST** $$

BEST TIME TO DRINK

1 year	5 years	10 years

FOOD PAIRINGS

charcuterie

grilled red meat

white meat

YOU MIGHT ALSO LIKE

Côtes du Rhône, Crozes-Hermitage, Languedoc-Roussillon

Also available in:
- white
- rosé

Ruby Cabernet (California)
supple and deeply colored

ORIGIN: UNITED STATES
California

VARIETALS   **COLOR**
 rubis cabernet

AROMAS
 red fruit jam   cherry   smoked

MOUTHFEEL

Tannins Firmness

1				5					10

Alcohol Heat

1				5					10

Acidity Crispness

1				5					10

SERVE AT 59-61°F **COST** $

BEST TIME TO DRINK

1 year		5 years						10 years

FOOD PAIRINGS

grilled red meat   white meat

charcuterie   roasted red meat

YOU MIGHT ALSO LIKE

Merlot (California), Cabernet Sauvignon (California), Côtes du Rhône, Languedoc Rouge

---

Saint-Émilion
robust and well-rounded

ORIGIN: FRANCE
Bordeaux (Libourne)

VARIETALS   **COLOR**
 merlot   cabernet franc   cabernet sauvignon

AROMAS
 blackcurrant   blackberry   prune

vanilla   coffee   undergrowth

MOUTHFEEL

Tannins Firmness

1				5					10

Alcohol Heat

1				5					10

Acidity Crispness

1				5					10

SERVE AT 61-64°F **COST** $$

BEST TIME TO DRINK

1 year		5 years						10 years

FOOD PAIRINGS

white meat   poultry

grilled red meat   roasted red meat

red meat with sauce

YOU MIGHT ALSO LIKE

Lussac-Saint-Émilion, Montagne-Saint-Émilion, Puisseguin-Saint-Émilion, Saint-Georges-Saint-Émilion, Lalande-de-Pomerol, Pécharmant

Saint-Joseph
well-rounded and velvety

ORIGIN: FRANCE
Northern Rhone Valley

VARIETALS   **COLOR**

 syrah

AROMAS

 blackcurrant   black pepper   licorice

MOUTHFEEL

Tannins Firmness

1	5	10

Alcohol Heat

1	5	10

Acidity Crispness

1	5	10

SERVE AT 61-64°F **COST** $$ to $$$

BEST TIME TO DRINK

1 year	5 years	10 years

FOOD PAIRINGS

 grilled red meat   red meat with sauce

 duck   white meat

 furred game   truffle

YOU MIGHT ALSO LIKE
rozes-Hermitage, IGP Ardèche Syrah, New World Syrah

Santenay
full-bodied and smooth

ORIGIN: FRANCE
Burgundy (Côte de Beaune)

VARIETALS   **COLOR**

 pinot noir

AROMAS

 raspberry   red currants   blueberry

violet   black pepper   cinnamon

MOUTHFEEL

Tannins Firmness

1	5	10

Alcohol Heat

1	5	10

Acidity Crispness

1	5	10

SERVE AT 59-61°F **COST** $$

BEST TIME TO DRINK

1 year	5 years	10 years

FOOD PAIRINGS

 grilled red meat   roasted red meat

 red meat with sauce   duck

furred game   feathered game

YOU MIGHT ALSO LIKE
Maranges, Rully, Mercurey, Chassagne-Montrachet, Pommard

Also available in:
● white

77

Also available in:
● white

Saumur-Champigny
robust and easy drinking

ORIGIN: FRANCE
Loire Valley (Anjou and Saumur)

VARIETALS

 cabernet franc

 cabernet sauvignon

COLOR

AROMAS

 raspberry — blackcurrant — red currants

licorice

MOUTHFEEL

Tannins Firmness

1   5   10

Alcohol Heat

1   5   10

Acidity Crispness

1   5   10

SERVE AT 🌡 57–61°F   COST $ to $$

BEST TIME TO DRINK

1 year   5 years   10 years

FOOD PAIRINGS

white meat

poultry

grilled red meat

red meat with sauce

desserts with red fruit

YOU MIGHT ALSO LIKE

Anjou, Anjou Villages, Anjou Villages Brissac, Saumur, Saint-Nicolas-de-Bourgueil, Bourgueil, Chinon

---

Shiraz Cabernet Sauvignon (South Eastern Australia)
supple and approachable

ORIGIN: AUSTRALIA
South Eastern Australia

VARIETALS

 syrah/shiraz

 cabernet sauvignon

COLOR

AROMAS

 black fruit jam

 black cherry

 smoked

spices

 blackberry

 wood

MOUTHFEEL

Tannins Firmness

1   5   10

Alcohol Heat

1   5   10

Acidity Crispness

1   5   10

SERVE AT 🌡 57–59°F   COST $ to $$

BEST TIME TO DRINK

1 year   5 years   10 years

FOOD PAIRINGS

barbecue

charcuterie

grilled red meat

white meat

YOU MIGHT ALSO LIKE

Côtes du Rhône Villages, Languedoc-Roussillon, Calatayud, Cariñena, Nero d'Avola (Sicily), Primitivo di Puglia

Shiraz (SE Australia)
supple and ripe

ORIGIN: AUSTRALIA
South Eastern Australia

VARIETALS
 syrah/shiraz

COLOR

AROMAS
blackberry · black fruit jam · mint

smoked · licorice · leather

MOUTHFEEL
Tannins Firmness

1	5	10

Alcohol Heat

1	5	10

Acidity Crispness

1	5	10

SERVE AT 57-59°F **COST** $ to $$

BEST TIME TO DRINK
1 year	5 years	10 years

FOOD PAIRINGS
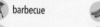 barbecue

 charcuterie

 grilled red meat

 white meat

YOU MIGHT ALSO LIKE
Côtes du Rhône Villages, Languedoc-Roussillon, Jecla, Jumilla, Primitivo di Puglia, Syrah (San Juan), Syrah (Swartland)

Tannat (Uruguay)
robust and fresh

ORIGIN: URUGUAY

VARIETALS
tannat

COLOR

AROMAS
blackcurrant · blackberry · licorice

leather · black pepper · mint

tobacco · undergrowth

MOUTHFEEL
Tannins Firmness

1	5	10

Alcohol Heat

1	5	10

Acidity Crispness

1	5	10

SERVE AT 59-61°F **COST** $$

BEST TIME TO DRINK
1 year	5 years	10 years

FOOD PAIRINGS
 charcuterie

 grilled red meat

 white meat

 poultry

YOU MIGHT ALSO LIKE
Madiran, Irouléguy, Tursan, Saint-Mont

Also available in:
● rosé

Touraine Rouge
robust and aromatic

ORIGIN: FRANCE
Loire Valley (Touraine)

VARIETALS **COLOR**

 malbec (côt)   cabernet franc

AROMAS

 raspberry   blackcurrant leather

MOUTHFEEL

Tannins Firmness

1				5					10

Alcohol Heat

1				5					10

Acidity Crispness

1				5					10

SERVE AT 🌡 57-61°F **COST** $

BEST TIME TO DRINK

1 year		5 years				10 years

FOOD PAIRINGS

white meat poultry

grilled red meat red meat with sauce

YOU MIGHT ALSO LIKE

Touraine-Amboise, Touraine-Chenonceaux, Valençay, Cheverny

Red Wines from Aragón
(Calatayud, Cariñena, Somontano, Campo de Borja)
supple and seductive

ORIGIN: SPAIN
Aragón

VARIETALS **COLOR**

 grenache   carignan

AROMAS

 raspberry strawberry black pepper

licorice caramel leather

toast

MOUTHFEEL

Tannins Firmness

1				5					10

Alcohol Heat

1				5					10

Acidity Crispness

1				5					10

SERVE AT 🌡 57-61°F **COST** $ to $$

BEST TIME TO DRINK

1 year		5 years				10 years

FOOD PAIRINGS

 grilled red meat white meat

 roasted red meat   barbecue

 charcuterie

YOU MIGHT ALSO LIKE

Côtes du Rhône, Languedoc-Roussillon, Côtes du Roussillon, Minervois, Corbières, Navarre, Catalunya

---

Also available in:

● white (excluding blends) (cross reference)

80

RED WINES: POWERFUL AND BALANCED

Aglianico del Vulture
intense and structured

ORIGIN: ITALY
Basilicata

VARIETALS

 aglianico

COLOR

AROMAS

 red plum

cherry

blackberry

leather

rose

smoked

wood

MOUTHFEEL

Tannins Firmness

1	5	10

Alcohol Heat

1	5	10

Acidity Crispness

1	5	10

SERVE AT 59–63°F **COST** $$ to $$$

BEST TIME TO DRINK

1 year	5 years	10 years

FOOD PAIRINGS

grilled red meat

roasted red meat

furred game

red meat with sauce

YOU MIGHT ALSO LIKE
Barolo, Barbaresco, Brunello di Montalcino, Taurasi

Amarone della Valpolicella
opulent and full-bodied

ORIGIN: ITALY
Veneto

VARIETALS

 corvina   corvinone   rondinella

COLOR

AROMAS

prune

cacao

dried fruit

black fruit jam

spices

wood

licorice

smoked

MOUTHFEEL

Tannins Firmness

1	5	10

Alcohol Heat

1	5	10

SERVE AT 59–63°F **COST** $$$ to $$$$$

BEST TIME TO DRINK

1 year	5 years	10 years

FOOD PAIRINGS

furred game

roasted red meat

red meat with sauce

YOU MIGHT ALSO LIKE
Zinfandel (Sonoma Valley), Châteauneuf-du-Pape, Priorat, Maury Sec

Bordeaux Blend (Alexander Valley)
complex and fleshy

ORIGIN: UNITED STATES
North Coast of California
Sonoma County

VARIETALS

 cabernet sauvignon   merlot   **COLOR** cabernet franc

AROMAS

 black cherry   blackcurrant   red plum

 mint   toast

MOUTHFEEL

Tannins Firmness
1   5   10
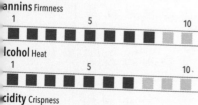

Alcohol Heat
1   5   10

Acidity Crispness
1   5   10

SERVE AT 59–61°F   **COST** \$\$\$ to \$\$\$\$\$

BEST TIME TO DRINK
1 year   10 years   20 years

FOOD PAIRINGS

 roasted red meat   grilled red meat

 duck   red meat with sauce

YOU MIGHT ALSO LIKE

Bordeaux-style blends (Stellenbosch), Bordeaux-style blends (Margaret River), Bolgheri, Haut-Médoc

---

Bairrada
firm and structured

ORIGIN: PORTUGAL
Beira Atlântico

VARIETALS

 baga   touriga nacional   **COLOR** alfrocheiro

AROMAS

 red plum   blackberry   blueberry

 wood   hay   tobacco

 smoked   leather

MOUTHFEEL

Tannins Firmness
1   5   10

Alcohol Heat
1   5   10

Acidity Crispness
1   5   10

SERVE AT 59–63°F   **COST** \$\$ to \$\$\$

BEST TIME TO DRINK
1 year   10 years   20 years

FOOD PAIRINGS

 grilled red meat   roasted red meat

red meat with sauce

YOU MIGHT ALSO LIKE

Langhe Nebbiolo, Saint-Mont, Madiran

Also available in:
○ white
○ rosé

Barbaresco
powerful and complex

ORIGIN: ITALY
Piedmont

VARIETALS

COLOR

 nebbiolo

AROMAS

 red plum   cherry   rose

violet   tobacco   truffle

licorice   wood

MOUTHFEEL

Tannins Firmness

| 1 | | | | 5 | | | | 10 |

Alcohol Heat

| 1 | | | | 5 | | | | 10 |

Acidity Crispness

| 1 | | | | 5 | | | | 10 |

SERVE AT 59-63°F   **COST** $$$ to $$$$$

BEST TIME TO DRINK

| 1 year | | | 10 years | | | | 20 years |

FOOD PAIRINGS

 grilled red meat   roasted red meat

 red meat with sauce

YOU MIGHT ALSO LIKE

Barolo, Brunello di Montalcino, vino nobile di Montepulciano, Bandol

Barolo
structured and complex

ORIGIN: ITALY
Piedmont

VARIETALS

COLOR

 nebbiolo

AROMAS

 red plum   cherry   rose

leather   mushrooms   licorice

MOUTHFEEL

Tannins Firmness

| 1 | | | | 5 | | | | 10 |

Alcohol Heat

| 1 | | | | 5 | | | | 10 |

Acidity Crispness

| 1 | | | | 5 | | | | 10 |

SERVE AT 61-64°F   **COST** $$ to $$$$$

BEST TIME TO DRINK

| 1 year | 10 years | 20 years | 30 years | 40 years |

FOOD PAIRINGS

 furred game   duck

 truffle   roasted red meat

 red meat with sauce

YOU MIGHT ALSO LIKE

Barbaresco, Langhe Nebbiolo, Brunello di Montalcino, Taurasi, Cahors

Bolgheri
full-bodied and terroir-driven

ORIGIN: ITALY
Tuscany

VARIETALS

cabernet sauvignon

merlot

sangiovese

petit verdot

COLOR
cabernet franc

AROMAS

blackcurrant

black fruit jam

vanilla

spices

toast

mint

MOUTHFEEL

Tannins Firmness

1	5	10

Alcohol Heat

1	5	10

Acidity Crispness

1	5	10

SERVE AT 61-64°F **COST** $$ to $$$$$

BEST TIME TO DRINK

1 year	5 years	10 years	15 years	20 years

FOOD PAIRINGS

duck

feathered game

grilled red meat

poultry

roasted red meat

YOU MIGHT ALSO LIKE

Cabernet Sauvignon (California), Pauillac, Saint-Estèphe, Cabernet Sauvignon (Coonawarra)

Also available in:
○ white
○ rosé

Brunello di Montalcino
powerful and complex

ORIGIN: ITALY
Tuscany

VARIETALS

brunello (variante du sangiovese)

COLOR

AROMAS

cherry

strawberry

blueberry

toast

spices

undergrowth

MOUTHFEEL

Tannins Firmness

1	5	10

Alcohol Heat

1	5	10

Acidity Crispness

1	5	10

SERVE AT 61-64°F **COST** $$ to $$$$$

BEST TIME TO DRINK

1 year	5 years	10 years	15 years	20 years

FOOD PAIRINGS

feathered game

roasted red meat

truffle

duck

furred game

YOU MIGHT ALSO LIKE

Chianti Classico, vino nobile di Montepulciano, Barolo, Barbaresco

Cabernet Sauvignon
(and blends),
Columbia Valley
intense and fleshy

ORIGIN: UNITED STATES

Washington
Columbia Valley

VARIETALS **COLOR**

 cabernet sauvignon   merlot

AROMAS

 blackberry black cherry toast

blackcurrant coffee mint

MOUTHFEEL

Tannins Firmness
1   5   10

Alcohol Heat
1   5   10

Acidity Crispness
1   5   10

SERVE AT 59-61°F **COST** $ to $$$$

BEST TIME TO DRINK
1 year   10 years   20 years

FOOD PAIRINGS

 roasted red meat   grilled red meat

 red meat with sauce   duck

YOU MIGHT ALSO LIKE

Cabernet Sauvignon (Coonawarra), Margaux, Saint-Julien, Haut-Médoc

Cabernet Sauvignon
(and blends),
Yakima Valley
excellent depth and complexity

ORIGIN: UNITED STATES

Washington
Yakima Valley

VARIETALS **COLOR**

 cabernet sauvignon

AROMAS

blackberry blackcurrant black cherry

mint smoked toast

spices

MOUTHFEEL

Tannins Firmness
1   5   10

Alcohol Heat
1   5   10

Acidity Crispness
1   5   10

SERVE AT 59-63°F **COST** $ to $$$$

BEST TIME TO DRINK
1 year   10 years   20 yea

FOOD PAIRINGS

 roasted red meat   grilled red meat

 red meat with sauce   duck

YOU MIGHT ALSO LIKE

Cabernet Sauvignon (Coonawarra), Margaux, Saint-Julien, Haut-Médoc

Also available in:
 rosé

Cabernet Sauvignon (Alexander Valley)
structured and powerful

ORIGIN: UNITED STATES
North Coast of California
Sonoma County

VARIETALS

 cabernet sauvignon

COLOR

AROMAS

 blackcurrant   black cherry   black fruit jam

toast   smoked   mint

MOUTHFEEL

Tannins Firmness

| 1 | 5 | 10 |

Alcohol Heat

| 1 | 5 | 10 |

Acidity Crispness

| 1 | 5 | 10 |

SERVE AT 59-61°F   **COST** $$$ to $$$$$

BEST TIME TO DRINK

| 1 year | 20 years | 40 years |

FOOD PAIRINGS

roasted red meat   grilled red meat

duck   red meat with sauce

YOU MIGHT ALSO LIKE

Cabernet Sauvignon (Stellenbosch, South Africa), Cabernet Sauvignon (Margaret River, Australia), Cabernet Sauvignon (Colchagua)

Cabernet Sauvignon and Merlot (Chile)
full-bodied and lively

ORIGIN: CHILE

VARIETALS

 cabernet sauvignon   merlot   Carménère

COLOR

AROMAS

 blackcurrant   cherry   blackberry

red bell pepper   mint   undergrowth

 toast

MOUTHFEEL

Tannins Firmness

| 1 | 5 | 10 |

Alcohol Heat

| 1 | 5 | 10 |

Acidity Crispness

| 1 | 5 | 10 |

SERVE AT 61-64°F   **COST** $$$

BEST TIME TO DRINK

| 1 year | 5 years | 10 years | 15 years | 20 years |

FOOD PAIRINGS

 duck   feathered game

 grilled red meat   poultry

 roasted red meat

YOU MIGHT ALSO LIKE

Cabernet Sauvignon (Stellenbosch, South Africa), Haut-Médoc, Listrac-Médoc, Cabernet Sauvignon (Margaret River, Australia), Bergerac

Also available in:
 rosé

Cabernet Sauvignon (Coonawarra)
elegant and lush

ORIGIN: AUSTRALIA
South Australia

VARIETALS
 cabernet sauvignon

COLOR

AROMAS
 blackcurrant
 blackberry
smoked

wood
 mint
toast

MOUTHFEEL
Tannins Firmness

1	5	10

Alcohol Heat

1	5	10

Acidity Crispness

1	5	10

SERVE AT 59–61°F   COST $$ to $$$$

BEST TIME TO DRINK

1 year	10 years	20 years

FOOD PAIRINGS
 grilled red meat
 roasted red meat

 duck
barbecue

YOU MIGHT ALSO LIKE
Cabernet Sauvignon (Stellenbosch, South Africa),
Cabernet Sauvignon (Mendoza), Passac-Léognan,
Saint-Julien

Cabernet Sauvignon (Margaret River)
intense and structured

ORIGIN: AUSTRALIA
Margaret River

VARIETALS
 cabernet sauvignon

COLOR

AROMAS
blackcurrant
toast
 mint

 red bell pepper
cherry

MOUTHFEEL
Tannins Firmness

1	5	10

Alcohol Heat

1	5	10

Acidity Crispness

1	5	10

SERVE AT 61–64°F   COST $$$

BEST TIME TO DRINK

1 year	5 years	10 years	15 years	20 years

FOOD PAIRINGS
 duck
 grilled red meat

feathered game
 poultry

YOU MIGHT ALSO LIKE
Cabernet Sauvignon (Stellenbosch, South Africa),
Haut-Médoc, Margaux, Saint-Julien, Listrac-Médoc,
Pauillac

Cabernet Sauvignon (Mendoza)
intense and structured

ORIGIN: ARGENTINA
Mendoza

VARIETALS
 cabernet sauvignon

COLOR

AROMAS
 blackcurrant black cherry toast

mint wood blueberry

MOUTHFEEL
Tannins Firmness

| 1 | | | | 5 | | | | | 10 |

Alcohol Heat

| 1 | | | | 5 | | | | | 10 |

Acidity Crispness

| 1 | | | | 5 | | | | | 10 |

SERVE AT 59-63°F **COST** $$ to $$$

BEST TIME TO DRINK

| 1 year | | | 10 years | | | | 20 years |

FOOD PAIRINGS
 grilled red meat roasted red meat

red meat with sauce barbecue

YOU MIGHT ALSO LIKE
Haut-Médoc, Cabernet Sauvignon (Margaret River, Australia), Cabernet Sauvignon (Stellenbosch, South Africa), Bolgheri

---

Cabernet Sauvignon (Napa Valley)
smooth and concentrated

ORIGIN: UNITED STATES
California
Napa Valley

VARIETALS
cabernet sauvignon

COLOR

AROMAS
blackcurrant  cherry cacao

vanilla black fruit jam mint

toast

MOUTHFEEL
Tannins Firmness

| 1 | | | | 5 | | | | | 10 |

Alcohol Heat

| 1 | | | | 5 | | | | | 10 |

Acidity Crispness

| 1 | | | | 5 | | | | | 10 |

SERVE AT 61-64°F **COST** $$ to $$$$$

BEST TIME TO DRINK

| 1 year | 10 years | 20 years | 30 years | 40 years |

FOOD PAIRINGS
 furred game red meat with sauce

roasted red meat truffle

YOU MIGHT ALSO LIKE
Cabernet Sauvignon (Argentina), Pauillac, Saint-Émilion Grand Cru Classé, Cabernet Sauvignon (Coonawarra), Blaye Côtes de Bordeaux

Also available in:
● rosé

Cabernet Sauvignon (Oakville)
structured and round

ORIGIN: UNITED STATES

North Coast of California
Napa Valley

VARIETALS
 cabernet sauvignon

COLOR

AROMAS
 blackcurrant
black fruit jam
 toast

 black cherry
smoked
mint

MOUTHFEEL

Tannins Firmness

1	5	10

Alcohol Heat

1	5	10

Acidity Crispness

1	5	10

SERVE AT 59-61°F **COST** $$$$ to $$$$$

BEST TIME TO DRINK

1 year	20 years	40 years

FOOD PAIRINGS
 roasted red meat
grilled red meat

 duck
 red meat with sauce

YOU MIGHT ALSO LIKE
Cabernet Sauvignon (Stellenbosch, South Africa),
Cabernet Sauvignon (Margaret River, Australia),
Pauillac, Saint-Julien

Cabernet Sauvignon (Paso Robles)
complex and structured

ORIGIN: UNITED STATES

Central Coast of California
Paso Robles

VARIETALS
 cabernet sauvignon

COLOR

AROMAS
blackcurrant
toast
black cherry

 undergrowth
mint
smoked

MOUTHFEEL

Tannins Firmness

1	5	10

Alcohol Heat

1	5	10

Acidity Crispness

1	5	10

SERVE AT 59-61°F **COST** $$ to $$$$

BEST TIME TO DRINK

1 year	10 years	20 years

FOOD PAIRINGS
 roasted red meat
grilled red meat

 red meat with sauce
furred game

YOU MIGHT ALSO LIKE
Cabernet Sauvignon (Coonawarra), Margaux,
Saint-Julien, Haut-Médoc

Cabernet Sauvignon (Rutherford)
complex and intense

ORIGIN: UNITED STATES
North Coast of California
Napa Valley

VARIETALS
 cabernet
sauvignon

COLOR

AROMAS

 blackcurrant
 black fruit jam
 toast

black cherry
smoked

MOUTHFEEL

Tannins Firmness

1	5	10

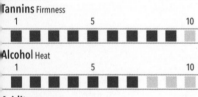

Alcohol Heat

1	5	10

Acidity Crispness

1	5	10

SERVE AT 59-61°F **COST** $$$$ to $$$$$

BEST TIME TO DRINK

1 year	20 years	40 years

FOOD PAIRINGS

 roasted red meat
 grilled red meat

 duck
 red meat with sauce

YOU MIGHT ALSO LIKE

Cabernet Sauvignon (Stellenbosch, South Africa),
Cabernet Sauvignon (Margaret River, Australia),
Pauillac, Saint-Julien

Cabernet Sauvignon (Santa Cruz Mountains)
structured and elegant

ORIGIN: UNITED STATES
Central Coast of California
Santa Cruz Mountains

VARIETALS
 cabernet
sauvignon

COLOR

AROMAS

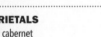 blackcurrant   blackberry   toast

smoked   undergrowth   mint

MOUTHFEEL

Tannins Firmness

1	5	10

Alcohol Heat

1	5	10

Acidity Crispness

1	5	10

SERVE AT 59-61°F **COST** $$$ to $$$$$

BEST TIME TO DRINK

1 year	10 years	20 years

FOOD PAIRINGS

 roasted red meat
 grilled red meat

duck
red meat with sauce

YOU MIGHT ALSO LIKE

Cabernet Sauvignon (Coonawarra), Margaux,
Saint-Julien, Haut-Médoc

Cabernet Sauvignon (Stags Leap District)
excellent depth and elegance

ORIGIN: UNITED STATES
North Coast of California
Napa Valley

VARIETALS
 cabernet sauvignon

COLOR

AROMAS
 blackcurrant
mint
toast
smoked
black cherry

MOUTHFEEL
Tannins Firmness

1	5	10

Alcohol Heat

1	5	10

Acidity Crispness

1	5	10

SERVE AT 59-61°F **COST** $$$ to $$$$

BEST TIME TO DRINK

1 year	20 years	40 years

FOOD PAIRINGS
 roasted red meat
 grilled red meat
duck
red meat with sauce

YOU MIGHT ALSO LIKE
Cabernet Sauvignon (Stellenbosch, South Africa),
Cabernet Sauvignon (Margaret River, Australia),
Pauillac, Saint-Julien

Cabernet Sauvignon (Stellenbosch)
structured and closed

ORIGIN: SOUTH AFRICA
Stellenbosch

VARIETALS
 cabernet sauvignon (blend)

COLOR

AROMAS
 blackcurrant
toast
mint
red bell pepper
smoked

MOUTHFEEL
Tannins Firmness

1	5	10

Alcohol Heat

1	5	10

Acidity Crispness

1	5	10

SERVE AT 61-64°F **COST** $$$

BEST TIME TO DRINK

1 year	10 years	20 years	30 years	40 years

FOOD PAIRINGS
 duck
 grilled red meat
 roasted red meat
 poultry

YOU MIGHT ALSO LIKE
Haut-Médoc, Saint-Julien, Passac-Léognan,
Cabernet Sauvignon (Margaret River, Australia)

Cabernet Sauvignon
and blends (Colchagua Valley)
powerful and jammy

ORIGIN: CHILE
Central Valley

VARIETALS   **COLOR**

 cabernet sauvignon   merlot   Carménère

AROMAS

- black cherry
- blackcurrant
- spices
- mint
- toast
- blackberry
- undergrowth
- licorice

MOUTHFEEL

Tannins Firmness

| 1 | | | | 5 | | | | | 10 |

Alcohol Heat

| 1 | | | | 5 | | | | | 10 |

Acidity Crispness

| 1 | | | | 5 | | | | | 10 |

SERVE AT 59–63°F   **COST** $ to $$$

BEST TIME TO DRINK

| 1 year | 10 years | 20 years |

FOOD PAIRINGS

- grilled red meat
- roasted red meat
- red meat with sauce
- furred game

YOU MIGHT ALSO LIKE

Cabernet Sauvignon (Stellenbosch, South Africa), Haut-Médoc, Saint-Julien, Pauillac, Cabernet Sauvignon (Sonoma), Cabernet Sauvignon (Margaret River, Australia)

Also available in:
 rosé

Cabernet Sauvignon
and blends (Maipo)
full-bodied and rich

ORIGIN: CHILE
Central Valley

VARIETALS   **COLOR**

 cabernet sauvignon   merlot   Carménère

AROMAS

- black cherry
- blackberry
- blackcurrant
- mint
- undergrowth
- spices
- wood
- smoked

MOUTHFEEL

Tannins Firmness

| 1 | | | | 5 | | | | | 10 |

Alcohol Heat

| 1 | | | | 5 | | | | | 10 |

Acidity Crispness

| 1 | | | | 5 | | | | | 10 |

SERVE AT 59–63°F   **COST** $ to $$$

BEST TIME TO DRINK

| 1 year | 10 years | 20 years |

FOOD PAIRINGS

- grilled red meat
- roasted red meat
- red meat with sauce
- furred game

YOU MIGHT ALSO LIKE

Cabernet Sauvignon (Stellenbosch, South Africa), Haut-Médoc, Saint-Julien, Cabernet Sauvignon (Napa Valley), Cabernet Sauvignon (Margaret River, Australia)

Also available in:
rosé

Cahors
muscular and deeply colored

ORIGIN: FRANCE
Southwest

VARIETALS

 malbec   merlot   tannat

COLOR

AROMAS

- blackberry
- prune
- violet
- blackcurrant
- cinnamon
- cacao
- truffle
- undergrowth

MOUTHFEEL

Tannins Firmness

| 1 | 5 | 10 |

Alcohol Heat

| 1 | 5 | 10 |

Acidity Crispness

| 1 | 5 | 10 |

SERVE AT 61-64°F   **COST** $$

BEST TIME TO DRINK

| 1 year | 5 years | 10 years |

FOOD PAIRINGS

- charcuterie
- duck
- feathered game
- roasted red meat
- grilled red meat
- mushrooms

YOU MIGHT ALSO LIKE

Madiran, Saint-Mont, Argentinian Malbec

Carménère
(Aconcagua Valley)
intense and fragrant

ORIGIN: CHILE
Aconcagua

VARIETALS

 Carménère

COLOR

AROMAS

- raspberry
- black cherry
- blackberry
- red fruit jam
- mint
- red bell pepper
- spices
- smoked

MOUTHFEEL

Tannins Firmness

| 1 | 5 | 10 |

Alcohol Heat

| 1 | 5 | 10 |

Acidity Crispness

| 1 | 5 | 10 |

SERVE AT 59-61°F   **COST** $$ to $$$

BEST TIME TO DRINK

| 1 year | 5 years | 10 years |

FOOD PAIRINGS

- grilled red meat
- roasted red meat
- red meat with sauce

YOU MIGHT ALSO LIKE

Merlot (Napa Valley), Pinotage (Stellenbosch), Malbec (Mendoza)

Carmignano
fruity and structured

Côte-Rôtie
dense and refined

ORIGIN: ITALY
Tuscany

ORIGIN: FRANCE
Northern Rhone Valley

VARIETALS

 sangiovese   cabernet sauvignon   canaiolo

 cabernet-franc

COLOR

VARIETALS

 syrah

COLOR

AROMAS

cherry   red plum   tea

blackcurrant   undergrowth   wood

AROMAS

blackberry   blueberry   blackcurrant

violet   black fruit jam   black pepper

tobacco   licorice

MOUTHFEEL

Tannins Firmness

1	5	10

Alcohol Heat

1	5	10

Acidity Crispness

1	5	10

MOUTHFEEL

Tannins Firmness

1	5	10

Alcohol Heat

1	5	10

Acidity Crispness

1	5	10

SERVE AT 59-62°F   **COST** $$ to $$$

BEST TIME TO DRINK

1 year	10 years	20 years

SERVE AT 59-63°F   **COST** $$$$

BEST TIME TO DRINK

1 year	5 years	10 years	15 years	20 years

FOOD PAIRINGS

 roasted red meat   red meat with sauce

 furred game   feathered game

FOOD PAIRINGS

grilled red meat   roasted red meat

red meat with sauce   duck

feathered game   furred game

YOU MIGHT ALSO LIKE

Brunello di Montalcino, Chianti Classico,
Montepulciano d'Abbruzzo

YOU MIGHT ALSO LIKE

Hermitage, Cornas, Saint-Joseph, Syrah (South Africa),
Shiraz (Victoria, Australia)

Douro
intense and full-bodied

ORIGIN: PORTUGAL
Douro

VARIETALS　**COLOR**

  blends

AROMAS

blackberry

black cherry

licorice

black pepper

toast

MOUTHFEEL

Tannins Firmness

| 1 | 5 | 10 |

Alcohol Heat

| 1 | 5 | 10 |

Acidity Crispness

| 1 | 5 | 10 |

SERVE AT 59-63°F　**COST** $$

BEST TIME TO DRINK

| 1 year | 5 years | 10 years | 15 years | 20 years |

FOOD PAIRINGS

red meat with sauce

roasted red meat

furred game

furred game

YOU MIGHT ALSO LIKE

Gigondas, Rasteau, Collioure, Priorat, Minervois La Livinière, Corbières-Boutenac

Etna
structured and fragrant

ORIGIN: ITALY
Sicily

VARIETALS　**COLOR**

 nerello mascalese nerello cappuccio

AROMAS

 Morello cherry

 raspberry

 tea

minerality

scrubland

MOUTHFEEL

Tannins Firmness

| 1 | 5 | 10 |

Alcohol Heat

| 1 | 5 | 10 |

Acidity Crispness

| 1 | 5 | 10 |

SERVE AT 57-61°F　**COST** $$ to $$$$

BEST TIME TO DRINK

| 1 year | 5 years | 10 years |

FOOD PAIRINGS

 roasted red meat

 grilled red meat

feathered game

barbecue

 Mediterranean cuisine

YOU MIGHT ALSO LIKE

Dolcetto d'Alba, Bierzo, Langhe Nebbiolo, Saint-Joseph, Mondeuse (Savoie), Bairrada

Also available in:
 white
 rosé

96

Also available in:
 white
rosé

Gevrey-Chambertin
structured, powerful

ORIGIN: FRANCE
Burgundy (Côte de Nuits)

VARIETALS

COLOR

pinot noir

AROMAS

strawberry | cherry | blackcurrant

violet | licorice | leather

undergrowth | vanilla

MOUTHFEEL

Tannins Firmness

| 1 | 5 | 10 |

Alcohol Heat

| 1 | 5 | 10 |

Acidity Crispness

| 1 | 5 | 10 |

SERVE AT 59-61°F **COST** $$$

BEST TIME TO DRINK

| 1 year | 5 years | 10 years | 15 years | 20 years |

FOOD PAIRINGS

grilled red meat | roasted red meat

red meat with sauce | duck

poultry | furred game

YOU MIGHT ALSO LIKE

Gevrey-Chambertin, Morey-Saint-Denis, Nuits-Saint-Georges, Corton

Haut-Médoc
dense and complex

ORIGIN: FRANCE
Bordeaux (Médoc)

VARIETALS

cabernet sauvignon | merlot | petit verdot

cabernet franc

COLOR

AROMAS

blackcurrant | blackberry | cherry

coffee | vanilla | cacao

toast

MOUTHFEEL

Tannins Firmness

| 1 | 5 | 10 |

Alcohol Heat

| 1 | 5 | 10 |

Acidity Crispness

| 1 | 5 | 10 |

SERVE AT 61-64°F **COST** $$ to $$$

BEST TIME TO DRINK

| 1 year | 5 years | 10 years | 15 years | 20 years |

FOOD PAIRINGS

white meat | poultry

grilled red meat | roasted red meat

duck | feathered game

YOU MIGHT ALSO LIKE

Listrac-Médoc, Margaux, Moulis-en-Médoc, Pauillac, Saint-Estèphe, Saint-Julien, Passac-Léognan, Pécharmant, Cahors

Hermitage
dense and refined

ORIGIN: FRANCE
Northern Rhone Valley

VARIETALS

 syrah

COLOR

AROMAS

 violet

blackberry

cherry

prune

black pepper

undergrowth

cacao

MOUTHFEEL

Tannins Firmness

1	5	10

Alcohol Heat

1	5	10

Acidity Crispness

1	5	10

SERVE AT 59-63°F **COST** $$$$ to $$$$$

BEST TIME TO DRINK

1 year	5 years	10 years	15 years	20 years

FOOD PAIRINGS

 grilled red meat

 roasted red meat

 red meat with sauce

 furred game

truffle

YOU MIGHT ALSO LIKE

Côte-Rôtie, Cornas, Saint-Joseph, Syrah (South Africa), Shiraz (Victoria, Australia)

Langhe Nebbiolo
firm and fruity

ORIGIN: ITALY
Piedmont

VARIETALS

nebbiolo

COLOR

AROMAS

 red plum

cherry

rose

violet

wood

undergrowth

licorice

MOUTHFEEL

Tannins Firmness

1	5	10

Alcohol Heat

1	5	10

Acidity Crispness

1	5	10

SERVE AT 59-63°F **COST** $$ to $$$$

BEST TIME TO DRINK

1 year	5 years	10 year

FOOD PAIRINGS

grilled red meat

 roasted red meat

red meat with sauce

Mediterranean cuisine

YOU MIGHT ALSO LIKE

Barolo, Barbaresco, Chianti Classico

Also available in:
 white

98

Madiran
dense and muscular

ORIGIN: FRANCE
Southwest

VARIETALS

 tannat

cabernet franc

cabernet sauvignon

fer-servadou

COLOR

AROMAS

 raspberry

blackcurrant

licorice

undergrowth

vanilla

MOUTHFEEL

Tannins Firmness

1	5	10

Alcohol Heat

1	5	10

Acidity Crispness

1	5	10

SERVE AT 61-64°F **COST** $ to $$

BEST TIME TO DRINK

1 year	5 years	10 years

FOOD PAIRINGS

grilled red meat

red meat with sauce

duck

furred game

feathered game

pressed cheese

YOU MIGHT ALSO LIKE
Saint-Mont, Irouléguy, Tursan, Tannat (Uruguay)

Malbec (Uco Valley)
intense and structured

ORIGIN: ARGENTINA
Mendoza

VARIETALS

malbec

COLOR

AROMAS

blackberry

blackcurrant

violet

licorice

toast

licorice

wood

MOUTHFEEL

Tannins Firmness

1	5	10

Alcohol Heat

1	5	10

Acidity Crispness

1	5	10

SERVE AT 59-61°F **COST** $$ to $$$

BEST TIME TO DRINK

1 year	10 years	20 years

FOOD PAIRINGS

grilled red meat

roasted red meat

furred game

red meat with sauce

YOU MIGHT ALSO LIKE
Yecla, Jumilla, Cahors, Châteauneuf-du-Pape, Bandol

Malbec (Mendoza)
powerful and fleshy

ORIGIN: ARGENTINA
Mendoza

. . . .

VARIETALS   **COLOR**

 malbec

. . . .

AROMAS

 blackberry   blackcurrant   smoked

licorice   spices   toast

peony   cacao

. . . .

MOUTHFEEL

Tannins Firmness
1   5   10

Alcohol Heat
1   5   10

Acidity Crispness
1   5   10

. . . .

SERVE AT 59-63°F **COST** $ to $$$$

BEST TIME TO DRINK
1 year   10 years   20 years

. . . .

FOOD PAIRINGS

 red meat with sauce   roasted red meat

 furred game   grilled red meat

. . . .

YOU MIGHT ALSO LIKE

Zinfandel (California), Côtes du Rhône Villages, Bandol, Toro

Margaux
dense and smooth

ORIGIN: FRANCE
Bordeaux (Médoc)

. . . .

VARIETALS   **COLOR**

 cabernet sauvignon   merlot   petit verdot

cabernet franc

. . . .

AROMAS

cherry   red currants   blackberry

cinnamon   undergrowth   vanilla

 coffee   cacao

. . . .

MOUTHFEEL

Tannins Firmness
1   5   10

Alcohol Heat
1   5   10

Acidity Crispness
1   5   10

. . . .

SERVE AT 61-64°F **COST** $$$ to $$$$

BEST TIME TO DRINK
1 year   10 years   20 years   30 years   40 years

. . . .

FOOD PAIRINGS

grilled red meat   roasted red meat

white meat   poultry

furred game   feathered game

. . . .

YOU MIGHT ALSO LIKE

Saint-Julien, Pauillac, Moulis-en-Médoc, Listrac-Médoc, Saint-Estèphe, Graves, Passac-Léognan

Merlot (Okanagan Valley)
fleshy and intense

ORIGIN: CANADA
British Columbia

VARIETALS

 merlot

 cabernet sauvignon

COLOR

AROMAS

red plum

black cherry

toast

wood

undergrowth

MOUTHFEEL

Tannins Firmness
1	5	10

Alcohol Heat
1	5	10

Acidity Crispness
1	5	10

SERVE AT 59-61°F **COST** $$ to $$$$

BEST TIME TO DRINK
1 year	10 years	20 years

FOOD PAIRINGS

 grilled red meat

roasted red meat

red meat with sauce

barbecue

poultry

YOU MIGHT ALSO LIKE
Médoc, Méritage (California), Bordeaux-style blends (Stellenbosch), Bordeaux-style blends (Central Valley, Chile)

Montepulciano d'Abruzzo
rich and full-bodied

ORIGIN: ITALY
Abruzzo

VARIETALS

montepulciano

COLOR

AROMAS

blackberry

red plum

black pepper

licorice

wood

black cherry

MOUTHFEEL

Tannins Firmness
1	5	10

Alcohol Heat
1	5	10

Acidity Crispness
1	5	10

SERVE AT 59-63°F **COST** $ to $$$

BEST TIME TO DRINK
1 year	5 years	10 years

FOOD PAIRINGS

 grilled red meat

roasted red meat

red meat with sauce

Mediterranean cuisine

YOU MIGHT ALSO LIKE
Chianti, Carmignano, Ribera del Duero, Cahors

Naoussa
structured and complex

ORIGIN: GREECE
Naoussa

VARIETALS

 Xynomavro

COLOR

AROMAS

 black cherry

 licorice

 blueberry

 licorice

leather

undergrowth

wood

smoked

MOUTHFEEL

Tannins Firmness

Alcohol Heat

Acidity Crispness

SERVE AT 59-63°F **COST** $$ to $$$

BEST TIME TO DRINK

1 year   10 years   20 years

FOOD PAIRINGS

grilled red meat   poultry

furred game

YOU MIGHT ALSO LIKE
Bairrada, Montepulciano d'Abbruzzo, Madiran, Cahors

Nemea
smooth and fleshy

ORIGIN: GREECE
Nemea

VARIETALS

 agiorgitiko

COLOR

AROMAS

red fruit jam

 raspberry

 scrubland

spices

wood

MOUTHFEEL

Tannins Firmness

1   5   10

Alcohol Heat

1   5   10

Acidity Crispness

1   5   10

SERVE AT 59-63°F **COST** $$ to $$$

BEST TIME TO DRINK

1 year   5 years   10 years

FOOD PAIRINGS

 grilled red meat   furred game

YOU MIGHT ALSO LIKE
Rioja, Langhe Nebbiolo, Ribera del Duero, Cairanne, Vacqueyras

Nuits-Saint-Georges
assertive and full-bodied

ORIGIN: FRANCE
Burgundy (Côte de Nuits)

VARIETALS

 pinot noir

COLOR

AROMAS

 cherry

strawberry

blackcurrant

rose

licorice

prune

vanilla

leather

MOUTHFEEL

Tannins Firmness

| 1 | | | | 5 | | | | | 10 |

Alcohol Heat

| 1 | | | | 5 | | | | | 10 |

Acidity Crispness

| 1 | | | | 5 | | | | | 10 |

SERVE AT 59-61°F **COST** $$$

BEST TIME TO DRINK

| 1 year | 5 years | 10 years | 15 years | 20 years |

FOOD PAIRINGS

grilled red meat

roasted red meat

red meat with sauce

duck

furred game

feathered game

YOU MIGHT ALSO LIKE

evrey-Chambertin, Fixin, Morey-Saint-Denis,
osne-Romanée, Beaune, Pommard

Also available in:

 white

103

Pauillac
excellent depth and density

ORIGIN: FRANCE
Bordeaux (Médoc)

VARIETALS

 cabernet sauvignon

 merlot

petit verdot

cabernet franc

COLOR

AROMAS

 blackcurrant

cherry

raspberry

vanilla

licorice

cinnamon

tobacco

mocha

MOUTHFEEL

Tannins Firmness

| 1 | | | | 5 | | | | | 10 |

Alcohol Heat

| 1 | | | | 5 | | | | | 10 |

Acidity Crispness

| 1 | | | | 5 | | | | | 10 |

SERVE AT 61-64°F **COST** $$$ to $$$$

BEST TIME TO DRINK

| 1 year | 10 years | 20 years | 30 years | 40 years |

FOOD PAIRINGS

grilled red meat

roasted red meat

duck

furred game

feathered game

cèpes

YOU MIGHT ALSO LIKE

Saint-Estèphe, Margaux, Moulis-en-Médoc,
Listrac-Médoc, Haut-Médoc, Passac-Léognan, Graves,
Cabernet Sauvignon (Margaret River, Australia)

Pessac-Léognan
powerful and complex

ORIGIN: FRANCE
Bordeaux (Graves)

VARIETALS

 cabernet sauvignon
 merlot
 petit verdot
cabernet franc

COLOR

AROMAS

 blackcurrant
blackberry
 violet
smoked
licorice
cacao
coffee
leather

MOUTHFEEL

Tannins Firmness

| 1 | | | | 5 | | | | | 10 |

Alcohol Heat

| 1 | | | | 5 | | | | | 10 |

Acidity Crispness

| 1 | | | | 5 | | | | | 10 |

SERVE AT 61-64°F **COST** $$$ to $$$$

BEST TIME TO DRINK

| 1 year | 10 years | 20 years | 30 years | 40 years |

FOOD PAIRINGS

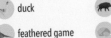 grilled red meat
roasted red meat
 duck
furred game
feathered game
poultry

YOU MIGHT ALSO LIKE

Pauillac, Saint-Estèphe, Saint-Julien, Haut-Médoc, Graves, Cabernet Sauvignon (Stellenbosch, South Africa)

Also available in:
● white

104

Pomerol
dense and velvety

ORIGIN: FRANCE
Bordeaux (Libourne)

VARIETALS

 merlot
cabernet franc

COLOR
cabernet sauvignon

AROMAS

 blackberry
 blackcurrant
 licorice
violet
truffle
cinnamon
coffee
leather

MOUTHFEEL

Tannins Firmness

| 1 | | | | 5 | | | | | 10 |

Alcohol Heat

| 1 | | | | 5 | | | | | 10 |

Acidity Crispness

| 1 | | | | 5 | | | | | 10 |

SERVE AT 61-64°F **COST** $$$$ to $$$$$

BEST TIME TO DRINK

| 1 year | 5 years | 10 years | 15 years | 20 years |

FOOD PAIRINGS

 grilled red meat
roasted red meat
duck
 feathered game
mushrooms
 pressed cheese

YOU MIGHT ALSO LIKE

Saint-Émilion Grand Cru, Lalande-de-Pomerol, Canon-Fronsac, Fronsac, Castillon, Francs Côtes de Bordeaux, Côtes de Bourg, Pécharmant

Pommard
robust and lively

ORIGIN: FRANCE
Burgundy (Côtes de Beaune)

VARIETALS   **COLOR**

 pinot noir

AROMAS

 cherry   red plum   blackberry

leather   black pepper   vanilla

coffee   cacao

MOUTHFEEL

Tannins Firmness

| 1 | | | | 5 | | | | | 10 |

Alcohol Heat

| 1 | | | | 5 | | | | | 10 |

Acidity Crispness

| 1 | | | | 5 | | | | | 10 |

SERVE AT 59-61°F   **COST** $$$

BEST TIME TO DRINK

| 1 year | | 5 years | | | | | | | 10 years |

FOOD PAIRINGS

 grilled red meat   roasted red meat

 red meat with sauce   duck

furred game   feathered game

YOU MIGHT ALSO LIKE
Corton, Nuits-Saint-Georges, Vosne-Romanée, Gevrey-Chambertin

Ribera del Duero (Reserva)
powerful and complex

ORIGIN: SPAIN
Castilla y León

VARIETALS   **COLOR**

 tempranillo

AROMAS

 blackberry   prune   leather

cinnamon   coffee   game

MOUTHFEEL

Tannins Firmness

| 1 | | | | 5 | | | | | 10 |

Alcohol Heat

| 1 | | | | 5 | | | | | 10 |

Acidity Crispness

| 1 | | | | 5 | | | | | 10 |

SERVE AT 61-64°F   **COST** $$ to $$$

BEST TIME TO DRINK

| 1 year | 5 years | 10 years | 15 years | 20 years |

FOOD PAIRINGS

furred game   red meat with sauce

roasted red meat   truffle

YOU MIGHT ALSO LIKE
Toro, Zinfandel (California), Gigondas, Bandol, Duoro

Saint-Émilion Grand Cru
dense and round

ORIGIN: FRANCE
Bordeaux (Libourne)

VARIETALS

 merlot   cabernet franc   **COLOR** cabernet sauvignon

AROMAS

 strawberry   cherry   blackberry

 prune   violet   vanilla

coffee   cacao

MOUTHFEEL

Tannins Firmness

1	5	10

Alcohol Heat

1	5	10

Acidity Crispness

1	5	10

SERVE AT 61-64°F **COST** $$$ to $$$$$

BEST TIME TO DRINK

1 year	5 years	10 years	15 years	20 years

FOOD PAIRINGS

 grilled red meat   roasted red meat

 red meat with sauce   duck

 feathered game   mushrooms

YOU MIGHT ALSO LIKE

Pomerol, Lalande-de-Pomerol, Fronsac, Canon-Fronsac, Castillon Côtes de Bordeaux, Pécharmant

---

Saint-Estèphe
powerful and complex

ORIGIN: FRANCE
Bordeaux (Médoc)

VARIETALS

 cabernet sauvignon   merlot   **COLOR** petit verdot

 cabernet franc

AROMAS

 blackcurrant   violet   blackberry

 licorice   vanilla   coffee

 cacao   almond

MOUTHFEEL

Tannins Firmness

1	5	10

Alcohol Heat

1	5	10

Acidity Crispness

1	5	10

SERVE AT 61-64°F **COST** $$$ to $$$$

BEST TIME TO DRINK

1 year	10 years	20 years	30 years	40 years

FOOD PAIRINGS

 grilled red meat   roasted red meat

duck   furred game

 feathered game   mushrooms

YOU MIGHT ALSO LIKE

Pauillac, Margaux, Listrac-Médoc, Moulis-en-Médoc, Haut-Médoc, Passac-Léognan, Graves

Saint-Julien
dense and velvety

ORIGIN: FRANCE
Bordeaux (Médoc)

VARIETALS
 cabernet sauvignon

 merlot

 petit verdot

 cabernet franc

COLOR

AROMAS
blueberry violet blackberry

prune cherry tobacco

cacao vanilla

MOUTHFEEL
Tannins Firmness

| 1 | | | | 5 | | | | | 10 |

Alcohol Heat

| 1 | | | | 5 | | | | | 10 |

Acidity Crispness

| 1 | | | | 5 | | | | | 10 |

SERVE AT 61–64°F **COST** \$\$\$ to \$\$\$\$

BEST TIME TO DRINK

| 1 year | 10 years | 20 years | 30 years | 40 years |

FOOD PAIRINGS
grilled red meat poultry

white meat roasted red meat

feathered game mushrooms

YOU MIGHT ALSO LIKE
Margaux, Pauillac, Saint-Estèphe, Moulis-en-Médoc, Listrac-Médoc, New World Cabernet Sauvignon

---

Shiraz (Hunter Valley)
concentrated and ripe

ORIGIN: AUSTRALIA
New South Wales

VARIETALS
 syrah/shiraz

COLOR

AROMAS
black fruit jam black cherry cacao

leather smoked wood

MOUTHFEEL
Tannins Firmness

| 1 | | | | 5 | | | | | 10 |

Alcohol Heat

| 1 | | | | 5 | | | | | 10 |

Acidity Crispness

| 1 | | | | 5 | | | | | 10 |

SERVE AT 57–61°F **COST** \$\$ to \$\$\$

BEST TIME TO DRINK

| 1 year | 5 years | 10 years |

FOOD PAIRINGS
furred game red meat with sauce

roasted red meat

YOU MIGHT ALSO LIKE
Shiraz (Barossa), Syrah (Swartland), Cornas, Syrah (Hunter Valley)

Shiraz and Blends (McLaren Vale)
opulent and concentrated

ORIGIN: AUSTRALIA
South Australia

VARIETALS

COLOR

 syrah/shiraz   grenache

AROMAS

 blackberry   red fruit jam   prune

cacao   licorice   smoked

wood   leather

MOUTHFEEL

Tannins Firmness

| 1 | | | | 5 | | | | | 10 |

Alcohol Heat

| 1 | | | | 5 | | | | | 10 |

Acidity Crispness

| 1 | | | | 5 | | | | | 10 |

SERVE AT 57–61°F   **COST** $$ to $$$

BEST TIME TO DRINK

| 1 year | 10 years | 20 years |

FOOD PAIRINGS

 grilled red meat   roasted red meat

furred game   red meat with sauce

YOU MIGHT ALSO LIKE

Shiraz (Barossa), Syrah (Swartland), Cornas, Gigondas, Châteauneuf-du-Pape, Cairanne

---

Shiraz (Barossa)
concentrated and fleshy

ORIGIN: AUSTRALIA
Barossa

VARIETALS

COLOR

 syrah

AROMAS

 blackberry   prune   cacao

licorice   smoked   black pepper

game

MOUTHFEEL

Tannins Firmness

| 1 | | | | 5 | | | | | 10 |

Alcohol Heat

| 1 | | | | 5 | | | | | 10 |

Acidity Crispness

| 1 | | | | 5 | | | | | 10 |

Sugar Sweetness

| 1 | | | | 5 | | | | | 10 |

SERVE AT 59–63°F   **COST** $ to $$$$$

BEST TIME TO DRINK

| 1 year | 10 years | 20 years | 30 years | 40 years |

FOOD PAIRINGS

 furred game   red meat with sauce

roasted red meat

YOU MIGHT ALSO LIKE

Syrah (Hunter Valley and McLaren Vale), Châteauneuf-du-Pape, Zinfandel (California), Bandol

Also available in:
rosé, sparkling (sparkling shiraz)

Taurasi
full-bodied and terroir-driven

ORIGIN: ITALY

Campania

VARIETALS

 aglianico

COLOR

AROMAS

red plum   rose   cherry

blackberry   leather   smoked

wood   spices

MOUTHFEEL

Tannins Firmness

1	5	10

Alcohol Heat

1	5	10

Acidity Crispness

1	5	10

SERVE AT 59-63°F   **COST** $$$ to $$$$

BEST TIME TO DRINK

1 year	10 years	20 years

FOOD PAIRINGS

 grilled red meat   roasted red meat

red meat with sauce   furred game

YOU MIGHT ALSO LIKE

Barolo, Barbaresco, Brunello di Montalcino, Aglianico del Vulture

---

Toro
ripe and concentrated

ORIGIN: SPAIN

Castilla y León

VARIETALS

tempranillo

COLOR

AROMAS

blackberry   prune   red fruit jam

coffee   wood   cacao

leather

MOUTHFEEL

Tannins Firmness

1	5	10

Alcohol Heat

1	5	10

Acidity Crispness

1	5	10

SERVE AT 59-63°F   **COST** $ to $$$$

BEST TIME TO DRINK

1 year	10 years	20 years

FOOD PAIRINGS

grilled red meat   roasted red meat

red meat with sauce   furred game

YOU MIGHT ALSO LIKE

Ribera del Duero, Priorat, Châteauneuf-du-Pape, Amarone, Bandol, Duoro

Also available in:
- blanc
- rosé

Vino Nobile di Montepulciano
powerful and firm

ORIGIN: ITALY
Tuscany

VARIETALS
 sangiovese

COLOR

AROMAS
 cherry   red plum   green herbs

tea   licorice   wood

undergrowth

MOUTHFEEL

Tannins Firmness

1	5	10

Alcohol Heat

1	5	10

Acidity Crispness

1	5	10

SERVE AT 59–63°F   **COST** $$ to $$$$

BEST TIME TO DRINK

1 year	10 years	20 years

FOOD PAIRINGS

 grilled red meat   roasted red meat

 red meat with sauce   furred game

YOU MIGHT ALSO LIKE

Brunello di Montalcino, Chianti Classico, Carmignano

RED WINES: RIPE AND SPICY

Bandol
powerful with excellent depth

ORIGIN: FRANCE
Provence

VARIETALS
 Mourvèdre   grenache   cinsault

COLOR

AROMAS
- blackberry
- blackcurrant
- undergrowth
- cinnamon
- licorice
- tobacco
- cacao

MOUTHFEEL

Tannins Firmness

| 1 | 5 | 10 |

Alcohol Heat

| 1 | 5 | 10 |

Acidity Crispness

| 1 | 5 | 10 |

SERVE AT 61–64°F COST $$

BEST TIME TO DRINK

| 1 year | 5 years | 10 years | 15 years | 20 years |

FOOD PAIRINGS
- grilled red meat
- roasted red meat
- red meat with sauce
- furred game

YOU MIGHT ALSO LIKE
Côtes de Provence, Coteaux Varois en Provence, Coteaux d'Aix-en-Provence, Minervois, Jumilla (Spain)

Also available in:
- white
- rosé

Cannonau di Sardegna
smooth and spicy

ORIGIN: ITALY
Sardinia

VARIETALS
grenache

COLOR

AROMAS
- red fruit jam
- red plum
- spices
- black pepper
- leather
- scrubland
- thyme

MOUTHFEEL

Tannins Firmness

| 1 | 5 | 10 |

Alcohol Heat

| 1 | 5 | 10 |

Acidity Crispness

| 1 | 5 | 10 |

SERVE AT 57–61°F COST $ to $$$

BEST TIME TO DRINK

| 1 year | 5 years | 10 years |

FOOD PAIRINGS
- roasted red meat
- grilled red meat
- Mediterranean cuisine
- barbecue

YOU MIGHT ALSO LIKE
Côtes du Rhône Villages, Vacqueyras, Cairanne, Rasteau, Calatayud, Cariñena

Also available in:
- rosé

Châteauneuf-du-Pape
rich and complex

ORIGIN: FRANCE

Southern Rhone Valley

VARIETALS

 grenache   syrah   Mourvèdre

cinsault

COLOR

AROMAS

cherry   blackcurrant   black pepper

scrubland   truffle   cinnamon

MOUTHFEEL

Tannins Firmness

| 1 | | | | 5 | | | | 10 |

Alcohol Heat

| 1 | | | | 5 | | | | 10 |

Acidity Crispness

| 1 | | | | 5 | | | | 10 |

SERVE AT 61-64°F   **COST** $$$

BEST TIME TO DRINK

| 1 year | 5 years | 10 years | 15 years | 20 years |

FOOD PAIRINGS

red meat with sauce   feathered game

furred game   truffle

Middle Eastern cuisine

YOU MIGHT ALSO LIKE

Gigondas, Vacqueyras, Rasteau, Beaumes de Venise, Lirac, Vinsobres, Côtes du Rhône Villages, Collioure

Also available in:
○ white

Corbières
round and peppery

ORIGIN: FRANCE

Languedoc

VARIETALS

 carignan   grenache   Mourvèdre

syrah

COLOR

AROMAS

blackcurrant   blackberry   black pepper

licorice   scrubland

MOUTHFEEL

Tannins Firmness

| 1 | | | | 5 | | | | 10 |

Alcohol Heat

| 1 | | | | 5 | | | | 10 |

Acidity Crispness

| 1 | | | | 5 | | | | 10 |

SERVE AT 57-61°F   **COST** $ to $$

BEST TIME TO DRINK

| 1 year | 5 years | 10 years |

FOOD PAIRINGS

grilled red meat   barbecue

duck   red meat with sauce

Mediterranean cuisine   mushrooms

YOU MIGHT ALSO LIKE

Corbières-Boutenac, Minervois, Minervois La Livinière, Saint-Chinian, Fitou, Faugères

Also available in:
○ white
○ rosé

Corsica or Vin de Corse
ripe and silky

ORIGIN: FRANCE
Corsica

VARIETALS

 grenache   niellucciu   Sciacarellu

COLOR

AROMAS

cherry black pepper licorice

leather

MOUTHFEEL

Tannins Firmness

| 1 | | | | 5 | | | | | 10 |

Alcohol Heat

| 1 | | | | 5 | | | | | 10 |

Acidity Crispness

| 1 | | | | 5 | | | | | 10 |

SERVE AT 57-61°F **COST** $$

BEST TIME TO DRINK

| 1 year | | | | 5 years | | | | | 10 years |

FOOD PAIRINGS

 grilled red meat   red meat with sauce

 white meat Mediterranean cuisine

 Middle Eastern cuisine

YOU MIGHT ALSO LIKE

Ajaccio, Patrimonio, Chianti Classico

Also available in:
● white
● rosé

Costières-de-Nîmes
round and velvety

ORIGIN: FRANCE
Rhone Valley

VARIETALS

 grenache   Mourvèdre   syrah

COLOR

AROMAS

cherry blackberry violet

black pepper

MOUTHFEEL

Tannins Firmness

| 1 | | | | 5 | | | | | 10 |

Alcohol Heat

| 1 | | | | 5 | | | | | 10 |

Acidity Crispness

| 1 | | | | 5 | | | | | 10 |

SERVE AT 57-61°F **COST** $

BEST TIME TO DRINK

| 1 year | | | | 5 years | | | | | 10 years |

FOOD PAIRINGS

 grilled red meat   red meat with sauce

white meat   poultry

 feathered game   Mediterranean cuisine

YOU MIGHT ALSO LIKE

Côtes du Rhône, Côtes du Rhône Villages, Duché d'Uzès, Côtes du Vivarais, Minervois, Côtes du Roussillon

Also available in:
● white
● rosé

Côtes du Rhône and Côtes du Rhône Villages
round and spicy

ORIGIN: FRANCE
Southern Rhone Valley

VARIETALS

grenache   syrah   Mourvèdre

COLOR

AROMAS

 red fruit jam   cherry   blueberry

licorice   black pepper

MOUTHFEEL

Tannins Firmness

1	5	10

Alcohol Heat

1	5	10

Acidity Crispness

1	5	10

SERVE AT 57-61°F   **COST** $ to $$

BEST TIME TO DRINK

1 year	5 years	10 years

FOOD PAIRINGS

grilled red meat   red meat with sauce

barbecue   Middle Eastern cuisine

YOU MIGHT ALSO LIKE

Costières de Nîmes, Côtes du Vivarais, Luberon, Ventoux, Duché d'Uzès, Coteaux de Pierrevert, Signan-les-Adhémar, Côtes du Roussillon, Languedoc-Roussillon, Reds from Aragon (Spain)

Also available in:
 white
 rosé

115

Côtes du Roussillon and Côtes du Roussillon Villages
dense and ripe

ORIGIN: FRANCE
Roussillon

VARIETALS

carignan   grenache   Mourvèdre

syrah

COLOR

AROMAS

 cherry   blackberry   blackcurrant

violet   scrubland   leather

MOUTHFEEL

Tannins Firmness

1	5	10

Alcohol Heat

1	5	10

Acidity Crispness

1	5	10

SERVE AT 57-61°F   **COST** $ to $$

BEST TIME TO DRINK

1 year	5 years	10 years

FOOD PAIRINGS

grilled red meat   red meat with sauce

furred game   Mediterranean cuisine

YOU MIGHT ALSO LIKE

Maury Sec, Collioure, Minervois, Corbières, Languedoc-Roussillon, Côtes du Rhône

Also available in:
 white (Côtes du Roussillon)
 rosé (Côtes du Roussillon)

Faugères
round and ripe

ORIGIN: FRANCE
Languedoc

VARIETALS

 grenache carignan syrah

carignan cinsault

COLOR

AROMAS

strawberry · blackcurrant · prune

red fruit jam · scrubland · leather

vanilla · coffee

MOUTHFEEL

Tannins Firmness
| 1 | 5 | 10 |

Alcohol Heat
| 1 | 5 | 10 |

Acidity Crispness
| 1 | 5 | 10 |

SERVE AT 61-64°F **COST** $

BEST TIME TO DRINK
| 1 year | 5 years | 10 years |

FOOD PAIRINGS

grilled red meat · red meat with sauce

furred game · feathered game

YOU MIGHT ALSO LIKE
Saint-Chinian, Languedoc-Roussillon, Minervois, Corbières, Fitou, Côtes du Roussillon Villages

Also available in:
● white
● rosé

Fitou
firm and lively

ORIGIN: FRANCE
Languedoc

VARIETALS

 carignan grenache Mourvèdre

syrah

COLOR

AROMAS

blackberry · raspberry · cherry

black pepper · vanilla · leather

MOUTHFEEL

Tannins Firmness
| 1 | 5 | 10 |

Alcohol Heat
| 1 | 5 | 10 |

Acidity Crispness
| 1 | 5 | 10 |

SERVE AT 61-64°F **COST** $

BEST TIME TO DRINK
| 1 year | 5 years | 10 years |

FOOD PAIRINGS

charcuterie · grilled red meat

red meat with sauce · furred game

duck · Middle Eastern cuisine

YOU MIGHT ALSO LIKE
Corbières, Corbières-Boutenac, Côtes du Roussillon Villages, Languedoc-Roussillon

Gigondas
structured and lively

ORIGIN: FRANCE
Southern Rhone Valley

VARIETALS
 grenache syrah Mourvèdre

COLOR

AROMAS
- cherry
- blackberry
- blackcurrant
- coffee
- cacao
- licorice
- leather

MOUTHFEEL

Tannins Firmness

1	5	10

Alcohol Heat

1	5	10

Acidity Crispness

1	5	10

SERVE AT 61-64°F **COST** $$

BEST TIME TO DRINK

1 year	5 years	10 years

FOOD PAIRINGS
- grilled red meat
- red meat with sauce
- duck
- feathered game
- furred game
- Middle Eastern cuisine

YOU MIGHT ALSO LIKE
Châteauneuf-du-Pape, Lirac, Vacqueyras, Vinsobres, Rasteau, Collioure

Also available in:
- rosé

Jumilla
spicy and ripe

ORIGIN: SPAIN
Levant

VARIETALS
 Monastrell (Mourvèdre) tempranillo grenache

COLOR

AROMAS
- black fruit jam
- prune
- licorice
- black pepper
- smoked
- wood
- game

MOUTHFEEL

Tannins Firmness

1	5	10

Alcohol Heat

1	5	10

Acidity Crispness

1	5	10

SERVE AT 59-63°F **COST** $$ to $$$

BEST TIME TO DRINK

1 year	5 years	10 years

FOOD PAIRINGS
- grilled red meat
- roasted red meat
- furred game
- red meat with sauce
- Mediterranean cuisine

YOU MIGHT ALSO LIKE
Bandol, Yecla, Zinfandel (Sonoma Valley), Syrah (Hunter Valley), Châteauneuf-du-Pape

Also available in:
- white
- rosé

Languedoc-Roussillon
round and intense

ORIGIN: FRANCE
Languedoc

VARIETALS

 grenache   Mourvèdre   syrah

COLOR

AROMAS

 raspberry   blackberry   blackcurrent

black pepper   scrubland   licorice

violet   leather

MOUTHFEEL

Tannins Firmness

| 1 | | | | 5 | | | | | 10 |

Alcohol Heat

| 1 | | | | 5 | | | | | 10 |

Acidity Crispness

| 1 | | | | 5 | | | | | 10 |

SERVE AT 59-63°F **COST** $$

BEST TIME TO DRINK

| 1 year | | | | 5 years | | | | | 10 years |

FOOD PAIRINGS

 white meat   grilled red meat

roasted red meat   red meat with sauce

duck   mushrooms

YOU MIGHT ALSO LIKE

Faugères, Saint-Chinian, Minervois, Corbières, Corbières-Boutenac, Côtes du Rhône Villages, Côtes du Roussillon Villages

Also available in:
 white
rosé

Minervois
powerful and intense

ORIGIN: FRANCE
Languedoc

VARIETALS

grenache   syrah   Mourvèdre

COLOR

AROMAS

 blackcurrant   violet   licorice

scrubland   cinnamon   vanilla

MOUTHFEEL

Tannins Firmness

| 1 | | | | 5 | | | | | 10 |

Alcohol Heat

| 1 | | | | 5 | | | | | 10 |

Acidity Crispness

| 1 | | | | 5 | | | | | 10 |

SERVE AT 59-63°F **COST** $ to $$

BEST TIME TO DRINK

| 1 year | | | | 5 years | | | | | 10 year |

FOOD PAIRINGS

 grilled red meat   red meat with sauce

duck   Middle Eastern cuisine

Middle Eastern cuisine

YOU MIGHT ALSO LIKE

Corbières, Languedoc-Roussillon, Faugères, Saint-Chinian, Côtes du Rhône Villages, Côtes du Roussillon Villages

Also available in:
white
rosé

Petite Sirah
(California)
spicy and atypical

ORIGIN: UNITED STATES
California

VARIETALS
 petite sirah
(durif)

COLOR

AROMAS
 black cherry
 blueberry
licorice
 black pepper
 cacao
tea
spices

MOUTHFEEL

Tannins Firmness

1				5				10

Alcohol Heat

1				5				10

Acidity Crispness

1				5				10

SERVE AT 65-70°F **COST** $ to $$

BEST TIME TO DRINK

1 year		5 years			10 years

FOOD PAIRINGS
 furred game
grilled red meat
 red meat with sauce
 duck

YOU MIGHT ALSO LIKE
Corbières, Minervois, Saint-Joseph

Also available in:
 rosé

Priorat
ripe with excellent depth

ORIGIN: SPAIN
Catalonia

VARIETALS
 grenache

COLOR

AROMAS
red fruit jam
cinnamon
 black pepper
leather
scrubland
prune

MOUTHFEEL

Tannins Firmness

1				5				10

Alcohol Heat

1				5				10

Acidity Crispness

1				5				10

Sugar Sweetness

1				5				10

SERVE AT 61-64°F **COST** $$ to $$$$

BEST TIME TO DRINK

1 year	5 years	10 years	15 years	20 years

FOOD PAIRINGS
furred game
red meat with sauce
roasted red meat
 truffle

YOU MIGHT ALSO LIKE
Châteauneuf-du-Pape, Gigondas, Zinfandel (California)

Also available in:
white
rosé

Rioja (Gran Reserva)
complex and graceful

Saint-Chinian
robusted and rounded

ORIGIN: SPAIN
Rioja

ORIGIN: FRANCE
Languedoc

VARIETALS
 tempranillo   grenache   mazuelo

graciano

COLOR

VARIETALS
grenache syrah Mourvèdre

COLOR

AROMAS
leather coffee dried fruit

mushrooms wood caramel

AROMAS
cherry blackcurrant raspberry

coffee cacao smoked

scrubland

MOUTHFEEL
Tannins Firmness

1	5	10

Alcohol Heat

1	5	10

Acidity Crispness

1	5	10

MOUTHFEEL
Tannins Firmness

1	5	10

Alcohol Heat

1	5	10

Acidity Crispness

1	5	10

SERVE AT 59-63°F **COST** $$$ to $$$$$

BEST TIME TO DRINK

1 year	10 years	20 years

SERVE AT 61-64°F **COST** $

BEST TIME TO DRINK

1 year	5 years	10 years

FOOD PAIRINGS
roasted red meat furred game

duck truffle

FOOD PAIRINGS
grilled red meat red meat with sauce

furred game Middle Eastern cuisine

YOU MIGHT ALSO LIKE
mature vintages of Grand Crus (Red) (Barolo, Pauillac, Saint-Estèphe, Hermitage, Châteauneuf-du-Pape, Taurasi, Cabernet Sauvignon from Stellenbosch)

YOU MIGHT ALSO LIKE
Faugères, Minervois, Corbières, Languedoc-Roussillon, Côtes du Rhône, Côtes du Rhône Villages, Côtes du Roussillon, Côtes du Roussillon Villages

Also available in:
● white
● rosé

Also available in:
● white
● rosé

Syrah (California)
spicy and supple

ORIGIN: UNITED STATES
California

VARIETALS

 syrah/shiraz

COLOR

AROMAS

blackberry   cacao   licorice

black pepper   spices   toast

MOUTHFEEL

Tannins Firmness

| 1 | 5 | 10 |

Alcohol Heat

| 1 | 5 | 10 |

Acidity Crispness

| 1 | 5 | 10 |

SERVE AT 57-61°F   **COST** $ to $$

BEST TIME TO DRINK

| 1 year | 5 years | 10 years |

FOOD PAIRINGS

 grilled red meat   roasted red meat

furred game   red meat with sauce

YOU MIGHT ALSO LIKE

Shiraz (Australia), Syrah (South Africa), Saint-Joseph, Crozes-Hermitage, Syrah (Argentina)

Syrah and Blends (Paso Robles)
intense and spicy

ORIGIN: UNITED STATES
Central Coast of California
Paso Robles

VARIETALS

 syrah/shiraz   grenache   Mourvèdre

 zinfandel

COLOR

AROMAS

blackberry   black fruit jam   black pepper

blackcurrant   toast   game

cacao

MOUTHFEEL

Tannins Firmness

| 1 | 5 | 10 |

Alcohol Heat

| 1 | 5 | 10 |

Acidity Crispness

| 1 | 5 | 10 |

SERVE AT 59-61°F   **COST** $$ to $$$$$

BEST TIME TO DRINK

| 1 year | 10 years | 20 years |

FOOD PAIRINGS

 roasted red meat   grilled red meat

furred game

YOU MIGHT ALSO LIKE

Shiraz (Barossa), Cornas, Hermitage, Syrah (South Africa)

Also available in:

● rosé

Syrah (Santa Lucia)
spicy and terroir-driven

ORIGIN: UNITED STATES
Central Coast of California
Monterey County

VARIETALS

 syrah/shiraz

COLOR

AROMAS

 blackberry

black fruit jam

black pepper

blackcurrant

toast

game

MOUTHFEEL

Tannins Firmness
1   5   10

Alcohol Heat
1   5   10

Acidity Crispness
1   5   10

SERVE AT 59-61°F **COST** $$$ to $$$$

BEST TIME TO DRINK
1 year   5 years   10 years

FOOD PAIRINGS

 roasted red meat

furred game

duck

red meat with sauce

YOU MIGHT ALSO LIKE

Shiraz (Barossa), Cornas, Hermitage,
Syrah (South Africa)

Syrah (Washington)
intense and spicy

ORIGIN: UNITED STATES
Washington

VARIETALS

 syrah/shiraz

COLOR

AROMAS

 blackberry

blackcurrant

black pepper

spices

smoked

leather

toast

MOUTHFEEL

Tannins Firmness
1   5   10

Alcohol Heat
1   5   10

Acidity Crispness
1   5   10

SERVE AT 59-61°F **COST** $$ to $$$$$

BEST TIME TO DRINK
1 year   5 years   10 year

FOOD PAIRINGS

 roasted red meat

grilled red meat

red meat with sauce

duck

YOU MIGHT ALSO LIKE

Saint-Joseph, Cornas, Crozes-Hermitage,
Syrah (Paso Robles)

Also available in:
 rosé

Syrah and Rhone-style Blends (Santa Rita Hills)
ripe and spicy

ORIGIN: UNITED STATES
Central Coast
Santa Barbara County

VARIETALS
 syrah/shiraz grenache

COLOR

AROMAS

 blackberry black cherry smoked

red fruit jam toast mint

spices

MOUTHFEEL

Tannins Firmness

| 1 | | | | 5 | | | | | 10 |

Alcohol Heat

| 1 | | | | 5 | | | | | 10 |

Acidity Crispness

| 1 | | | | 5 | | | | | 10 |

SERVE AT 59-61°F **COST** $$$ to $$$$$

BEST TIME TO DRINK

| 1 year | | | | 10 years | | | | | 20 years |

FOOD PAIRINGS

 grilled red meat   feathered game

white meat   furred game

YOU MIGHT ALSO LIKE

Châteauneuf-du-Pape, Gigondas, Shiraz (Australia)

Syrah (South African)
ripe and intense

ORIGIN: SOUTH AFRICA

VARIETALS
 syrah/shiraz

COLOR

AROMAS

blackberry   black fruit jam   licorice

cacao   spices   leather

MOUTHFEEL

Tannins Firmness

| 1 | | | | 5 | | | | | 10 |

Alcohol Heat

| 1 | | | | 5 | | | | | 10 |

Acidity Crispness

| 1 | | | | 5 | | | | | 10 |

SERVE AT 59-61°F **COST** $ to $$$

BEST TIME TO DRINK

| 1 year | | | 5 years | | | | | 10 years |

FOOD PAIRINGS

 grilled red meat   roasted red meat

 furred game   red meat with sauce

YOU MIGHT ALSO LIKE

Shiraz (Australia), Syrah (Argentina), Saint-Joseph, Crozes-Hermitage

Syrah (San Juan)
fragrant and juicy

ORIGIN: ARGENTINA
San Juan

VARIETALS
COLOR

 syrah/shiraz

AROMAS

 blackberry black fruit jam licorice

 spices black pepper cacao

MOUTHFEEL

Tannins Firmness

1	5	10

Alcohol Heat

1	5	10

Acidity Crispness

1	5	10

SERVE AT 59–61°F **COST** $ to $$

BEST TIME TO DRINK

1 year	5 years	10 years

FOOD PAIRINGS

 grilled red meat   roasted red meat

 furred game   red meat with sauce

YOU MIGHT ALSO LIKE
Shiraz (Barossa), Syrah (Swartland), Cornas, Syrah (Hunter Valley)

Syrah (Santa Ynez Valley)
fleshy and peppery

ORIGIN: UNITED STATES
Central Coast of California
Santa Barbara County

VARIETALS
COLOR

 syrah/shiraz

AROMAS

 blackberry black cherry black pepper

 licorice cacao toast

MOUTHFEEL

Tannins Firmness

1	5	10

Alcohol Heat

1	5	10

Acidity Crispness

1	5	10

SERVE AT 59–61°F **COST** $$$ to $$$$$

BEST TIME TO DRINK

1 year	5 years	10 year

FOOD PAIRINGS

 furred game   red meat with sauce

 roasted red meat   duck

YOU MIGHT ALSO LIKE
Shiraz (Barossa), Cornas, Hermitage, Syrah (South Africa)

Also available in:
● rosé

Syrah (Swartland)
fleshy and spicy

ORIGIN: SOUTH AFRICA
Coastal Region

VARIETALS

 syrah/shiraz

COLOR

AROMAS

blackberry | black fruit jam | licorice
cacao | spices | smoked
toast | game

MOUTHFEEL

Tannins Firmness

1	5	10

Alcohol Heat

1	5	10

Acidity Crispness

1	5	10

SERVE AT 59-61°F   **COST** $ to $$

BEST TIME TO DRINK

1 year	5 years	10 years

FOOD PAIRINGS

grilled red meat | roasted red meat
furred game | red meat with sauce

YOU MIGHT ALSO LIKE

Shiraz (Barossa), Syrah (California), Syrah (Argentina), Châteauneuf-du-Pape

Yecla
powerful and ripe

ORIGIN: SPAIN
Levante region

VARIETALS

 Monastrell (Mourvèdre)

COLOR

AROMAS

black fruit jam | raisin | red fruit jam
spices | smoked | scrubland

MOUTHFEEL

Tannins Firmness

1	5	10

Alcohol Heat

1	5	10

Acidity Crispness

1	5	10

SERVE AT 59-63°F   **COST** $ to $$

BEST TIME TO DRINK

1 year	5 years	10 years

FOOD PAIRINGS

grilled red meat | roasted red meat
furred game | red meat with sauce
Mediterranean cuisine

YOU MIGHT ALSO LIKE

Bandol, Jumilla, Zinfandel (Sonoma Valley), Syrah (Hunter Valley), Châteauneuf-du-Pape

Also available in:
● white
● rosé

Zinfandel (California)
supple and spicy

ORIGIN: UNITED STATES
California

VARIETALS   **COLOR**
 zinfandel

AROMAS
 black fruit jam   red fruit jam   prune

licorice   cinnamon   leather

smoked

MOUTHFEEL

Tannins Firmness
| 1 | | | | 5 | | | | | 10 |

Alcohol Heat
| 1 | | | | 5 | | | | | 10 |

Acidity Crispness
| 1 | | | | 5 | | | | | 10 |

SERVE AT 59–65°F   **COST** $ to $$

BEST TIME TO DRINK
| 1 year | | | | 5 years | | | | | 10 years |

FOOD PAIRINGS
 furred game   red meat with sauce

 roasted red meat   barbecue

YOU MIGHT ALSO LIKE
Côtes du Rhône Villages, Cairanne, Vacqueyras, Shiraz (Southern Australia), Languedoc-Roussillon

Also available in:
 rosé

Zinfandel (Dry Creek Valley)
smooth and full-bodied

ORIGIN: UNITED STATES
North Coast of California
Sonoma County

VARIETALS   **COLOR**
zinfandel

AROMAS
 prune   blackberry   black fruit jam

leather   licorice   black pepper

 game

MOUTHFEEL

Tannins Firmness
| 1 | | | | 5 | | | | | 10 |

Alcohol Heat
| 1 | | | | 5 | | | | | 10 |

Acidity Crispness
| 1 | | | | 5 | | | | | 10 |

SERVE AT 59–61°F   **COST** $$ to $$$

BEST TIME TO DRINK
| 1 year | | | | 5 years | | | | | 10 years |

FOOD PAIRINGS
furred game   roasted red meat

red meat with sauce   grilled red meat

YOU MIGHT ALSO LIKE
Châteauneuf-du-Pape, Gigondas, Primitivo di Puglia, Shiraz (Australia), Vacqueyras

Also available in:
rosé

Zinfandel (Lodi)
concentrated and opulent

ORIGIN: UNITED STATES

California Central Valley
Lodi

VARIETALS

COLOR

zinfandel

AROMAS

prune

smoked

candied fruit

leather

licorice

game

toast

MOUTHFEEL

Tannins Firmness
1			5					10	

Alcohol Heat
1			5					10	

Acidity Crispness
1			5					10	

SERVE AT 57-61°F **COST** $ to $$$

BEST TIME TO DRINK
1 year			10 years					20 years

FOOD PAIRINGS

red meat with sauce

furred game

roasted red meat

grilled red meat

YOU MIGHT ALSO LIKE

Châteauneuf-du-Pape, Gigondas, Primitivo di Puglia, Shiraz (Australia), Vacqueyras

Also available in:
rosé

Zinfandel (Sonoma)
concentrated and spicy

ORIGIN: UNITED STATES

North Coast of California
Sonoma County

VARIETALS

COLOR

zinfandel

AROMAS

prune

candied fruit

leather

licorice

black pepper

game

fig

MOUTHFEEL

Tannins Firmness
1			5					10

Alcohol Heat
1			5					10

Acidity Crispness
1			5					10

SERVE AT 57-61°F **COST** $$ to $$$

BEST TIME TO DRINK
1 year			5 years					10 years

FOOD PAIRINGS

furred game

red meat with sauce

grilled red meat

YOU MIGHT ALSO LIKE

Châteauneuf-du-Pape, Gigondas, Primitivo di Puglia, Shiraz (Australia), Vacqueyras

Also available in:
rosé

Zinfandel (Sonoma Valley)
brambly and ripe

ORIGIN: UNITED STATES
California Sonoma Valley

VARIETALS
 zinfandel

COLOR

AROMAS

 black fruit jam

prune

cinnamon

 black pepper

licorice

scrubland

 black olive

MOUTHFEEL

Tannins Firmness

1	5	10

Alcohol Heat

1	5	10

Acidity Crispness

1	5	10

Sugar Sweetness

1	5	10

SERVE AT 61-64°F   COST $$$

BEST TIME TO DRINK

1 year	10 years	20 years

FOOD PAIRINGS

 furred game

red meat with sauce

 roasted red meat

YOU MIGHT ALSO LIKE
Bandol, Priorat, Primitivo (Italy), Châteauneuf-du-Pape

Also available in:
● rosé

128

RED WINES:
SWEET

Ruby Port
juicy and ripe

ORIGIN: PORTUGAL
Douro

VARIETALS

- touriga nacional
- tinto cão
- tinta roriz
- tinta barroca
- touriga franca
- tinta amarela

COLOR

AROMAS

- black cherry
- blackberry
- black fruit jam
- black pepper
- cinnamon

MOUTHFEEL

Tannins Firmness
1   5   10

Alcohol Heat
1   5   10

Acidity Crispness
1   5   10

Sugar Sweetness
1   5   10

SERVE AT 59–61°F   **COST** $$ to $$$

BEST TIME TO DRINK
1 year   5 years   10 years

FOOD PAIRINGS

- chocolate desserts
- desserts with red fruit

YOU MIGHT ALSO LIKE

Rivesaltes, Maury Grenat, Banyuls Rimage

Tawny Port
smooth and complex

ORIGIN: PORTUGAL
Porto

VARIETALS

 blends

COLOR

AROMAS

- coffee
- walnut
- honey
- smoked
- candied fruit
- tobacco
- leather

MOUTHFEEL

Tannins Firmness
1   5   10

Alcohol Heat
1   5   10

Acidity Crispness
1   5   10

Sugar Sweetness
1   5   10

SERVE AT 59–61°F   **COST** $$ to $$$

BEST TIME TO DRINK
1 year   10 years   20 years

FOOD PAIRINGS

- blue cheese
- chocolate desserts
- desserts with red fruit

YOU MIGHT ALSO LIKE

Banyuls Grand Cru, Banyuls Traditionnel, Maury Tuilé,
Rivesaltes Tuilé, Rivesaltes Hors d'Âge

Vintage Port
opulent and full-bodied

ORIGIN: PORTUGAL
Porto

VARIETALS

 blends

COLOR

AROMAS

 black cherry   blackberry   black fruit jam

red fruit jam   cinnamon   black pepper

cacao   leather

MOUTHFEEL

Tannins Firmness

1	5	10

Alcohol Heat

1	5	10

Acidity Crispness

1	5	10

Sugar Sweetness

1	5	10

SERVE AT 59–61°F   **COST** $$$ to $$$$$

BEST TIME TO DRINK

1 year	10 years	20 years	30 years	40 years	50 years

FOOD PAIRINGS

 blue cheese   chocolate desserts

desserts with red fruit

YOU MIGHT ALSO LIKE

Rivesaltes, Maury Grenat, Banyuls Rimage

Recioto della Valpolicella
complex and lush

ORIGIN: ITALY
Veneto

VARIETALS

 corvina   corvinone   rondinella

COLOR

AROMAS

 raisin   prune   candied fruit

dried fruit   smoked   spices

honey

MOUTHFEEL

Tannins Firmness

1	5	10

Alcohol Heat

1	5	10

Acidity Crispness

1	5	10

Sugar Sweetness

1	5	10

SERVE AT 50–54°F   **COST** $$$ to $$$$$$

BEST TIME TO DRINK

1 year	10 years	20 years

FOOD PAIRINGS

 blue cheese   yellow fruit desserts

desserts with red fruit   chocolate desserts

YOU MIGHT ALSO LIKE

Vino Santo, Vin de Paille (Jura)

Sweet Red Wine Blends (California)
supple and sweet

ORIGIN: UNITED STATES
California

VARIETALS

 merlot

 ruby cabernet

zinfandel

COLOR

AROMAS

raspberry

red plum

cherry

red fruit jam

spices

MOUTHFEEL

Alcohol Heat

1	5	10
■■■□□□□□□□		

Acidity Crispness

1	5	10
■■■■□□□□□□		

Sugar Sweetness

1	5	10
■■■■□□□□□□		

SERVE AT 54–57°F **COST** $ to $$

BEST TIME TO DRINK

1 year	5 years	10 years
■■■■□□□□□□		

FOOD PAIRINGS

 aperitif

chocolate desserts

desserts with red fruit

YOU MIGHT ALSO LIKE
Porto, Rasteau, Banyuls

Vins Doux Naturels Grenat (Banyuls, Rivesaltes, Maury, Rasteau)
sweet and structured

ORIGIN: FRANCE
Roussillon

VARIETALS

grenache noir

COLOR

AROMAS

cherry

blackberry

black pepper

cacao

MOUTHFEEL

Tannins Firmness

1	5	10
■■■■■■■■□□		

Alcohol Heat

1	5	10
■■■■■■□□□□		

Acidity Crispness

1	5	10
■■■□□□□□□□		

Sugar Sweetness

1	5	10
■■■■■□□□□□		

SERVE AT 59–61°F **COST** $$

BEST TIME TO DRINK

1 year	10 years	20 years	30 years	40 years
■■■■■■■■□□				

FOOD PAIRINGS

duck

blue cheese

chocolate desserts

desserts with red fruit

YOU MIGHT ALSO LIKE
Ruby or Vintage Port

Also available in:
● white
● rosé

Vins Doux Naturels
Tuilés (Banyuls, Rivesaltes, Maury, Rasteau)
ripe and complex

ORIGIN: FRANCE
Roussillon

VARIETALS
grenache noir

COLOR

AROMAS

- prune
- fig
- coffee
- cacao
- leather
- walnut

MOUTHFEEL

Tannins Firmness

1	5	10

Alcohol Heat

1	5	10

Acidity Crispness

1	5	10

Sugar Sweetness

1	5	10

SERVE AT 59-61°F **COST** $$

BEST TIME TO DRINK

1 year	10 years	20 years	30 years	40 years

FOOD PAIRINGS

- foie gras
- blue cheese
- chocolate desserts

YOU MIGHT ALSO LIKE
Reserve Tawny Port

Also available in:
- white
- rosé

133

ROSÉ WINES

Bandol
dense and delicate

ORIGIN: FRANCE
Provence

VARIETALS

 Mourvèdre grenache cinsault

COLOR

syrah carignan

AROMAS

white flowers   citrus fruits   yellow peach

strawberry   exotic fruit   apricot

MOUTHFEEL

Alcohol Heat

1				5				10

Acidity Crispness

1				5				10

SERVE AT 46-50°F **COST** $$

BEST TIME TO DRINK

1 year		5 years			10 years

FOOD PAIRINGS

crustaceans (small)   grilled fish

Mediterranean cuisine   Middle Eastern cuisine

YOU MIGHT ALSO LIKE

Côtes de Provence, Coteaux Varois en Provence, Coteaux d'Aix-en-Provence

Bardolino Chiaretto
lively and fresh

ORIGIN: ITALY
Piedmont

VARIETALS

corvina   corvinone   rondinella

COLOR

AROMAS

raspberry   red currants   fruit candy

citrus fruits

MOUTHFEEL

Alcohol Heat

1				5				10

Acidity Crispness

1				5				10

SERVE AT 48-52°F **COST** $ to $$

BEST TIME TO DRINK

1 year		5 years			10 years

FOOD PAIRINGS

charcuterie   barbecue

aperitif   grilled fish

shellfish

YOU MIGHT ALSO LIKE

Rosé (Corsica), Rosé (Bordeaux), Rosé (Beaujolais)

Bordeaux Rosé
fleshy and fruity

ORIGIN: FRANCE
Bordeaux (regional appellations)

VARIETALS   **COLOR**

 cabernet sauvignon   merlot   cabernet franc

AROMAS

 strawberry   raspberry   cherry

blackcurrant   violet

MOUTHFEEL

Alcohol Heat
1   5   10

Acidity Crispness
1   5   10

SERVE AT 46–50°F   **COST** $

BEST TIME TO DRINK
1 year   5 years   10 years

FOOD PAIRINGS

 aperitif   charcuterie

 quiches and savory tarts   barbecue

 poultry   Chinese cuisine

YOU MIGHT ALSO LIKE
Bergerac, Côtes du Marmandais, Côtes de Duras, Buzet

Corsica or Vin-de-Corse
straightforward and spicy

ORIGIN: FRANCE
Corsica

VARIETALS   **COLOR**

 grenache   niellucciu   sciaccarellu

AROMAS

red currants   strawberry   white flowers

black pepper   citrus fruits

MOUTHFEEL

Alcohol Heat
1   5   10

Acidity Crispness
1   5   10

SERVE AT 46–50°F   **COST** $$

BEST TIME TO DRINK
1 year   5 years   10 years

FOOD PAIRINGS

 aperitif   Mediterranean cuisine

 barbecue   white meat

 Middle Eastern cuisine   Chinese cuisine

YOU MIGHT ALSO LIKE
Ajaccio, Patrimonio

Also available in:
● red
○ white

137

Also available in:
● red
○ white

Coteaux d'Aix-en-Provence
supple and fruity

ORIGIN: FRANCE
Provence

VARIETALS   **COLOR**

 grenache   counoise   cinsault

Mourvèdre   syrah

AROMAS

strawberry   yellow peach   apricot

white flowers   citrus fruits   exotic fruit

MOUTHFEEL

Alcohol Heat

1	5	10

Acidity Crispness

1	5	10

SERVE AT 46–50°F   **COST** $

BEST TIME TO DRINK

1 year	5 years	10 years

FOOD PAIRINGS

aperitif   Mediterranean cuisine

barbecue   white meat

Middle Eastern cuisine   Chinese cuisine

YOU MIGHT ALSO LIKE

Côtes de Provence, Bandol, Coteaux Varois en Provence

Also available in:
- red
- white

Côtes de Provence
round and fruity

ORIGIN: FRANCE
Provence

VARIETALS   **COLOR**

 grenache   syrah   cinsault

 tibouren

AROMAS

white flowers   yellow peach   apricot

strawberry   citrus fruits   exotic fruit

scrubland

MOUTHFEEL

Alcohol Heat

1	5	10

Acidity Crispness

1	5	10

SERVE AT 46–50°F   **COST** $

BEST TIME TO DRINK

1 year	5 years	10 years

FOOD PAIRINGS

 aperitif   Mediterranean cuisine

 barbecue   white meat

 Middle Eastern cuisine   Chinese cuisine

YOU MIGHT ALSO LIKE

Coteaux d'Aix-en-Provence, Coteaux Varois en Provence, Bandol, Corsican Wine

Also available in:
- red
- white

Languedoc-Roussillon
full-bodied and round

ORIGIN: FRANCE
Languedoc

VARIETALS   **COLOR**

 grenache   syrah   cinsault

Mourvèdre

AROMAS

cherry   strawberry   raspberry

white
flowers   citrus fruits

MOUTHFEEL

Alcohol Heat

1	5	10

Acidity Crispness

1	5	10

SERVE AT 46-50°F   **COST** $$

BEST TIME TO DRINK

1 year	5 years	10 years

FOOD PAIRINGS

aperitif   Mediterranean
cuisine

white meat   Middle Eastern
cuisine

Chinese cuisine

YOU MIGHT ALSO LIKE

Corbières, Cabardès, Côtes du Rhône, Costières de
Nîmes, Côtes du Roussillon

Also available in:
- red
- white

Navarra
supple and fruity

ORIGIN: SPAIN
Navarra

VARIETALS   **COLOR**

 grenache   tempranillo

AROMAS

strawberry   raspberry   red
currants

citrus fruits   fruit candy

MOUTHFEEL

Alcohol Heat

1	5	10

Acidity Crispness

1	5	10

SERVE AT 46-50°F   **COST** $$ to $$$

BEST TIME TO DRINK

1 year	5 years	10 years

FOOD PAIRINGS

aperitif   charcuterie

barbecue   grilled fish

Mediterranean
cuisine

YOU MIGHT ALSO LIKE

Coteaux d'Aix-en-Provence Rosé, Côtes de Provence
Rosé, Bandol Rosé, Rosé (Corsica), Tavel

Also available in:
- white
- red

Rosé d'Anjou and Rosé de Loire
bright and fruity

ORIGIN: FRANCE
Loire Valley

VARIETALS
 cabernet franc
 cabernet sauvignon
 pineau d'Aunis

 gamay
 malbec
 grolleau

COLOR

AROMAS
white flowers
raspberry
cherry

yellow peach
fruit candy

MOUTHFEEL
Alcohol Heat

| 1 | | 5 | | | 10 |

Acidity Crispness

| 1 | | 5 | | | 10 |

SERVE AT 🌡 46–50°F **COST** $

BEST TIME TO DRINK

| 1 year | 5 years | 10 years |

FOOD PAIRINGS
aperitif
charcuterie

quiches and savory tarts
white meat

desserts with red fruit

YOU MIGHT ALSO LIKE
Rosé de Loire, IGP Val de Loire

White Zinfandel (California)
soft and fruity

ORIGIN: UNITED STATES
California

VARIETALS
zinfandel

COLOR

AROMAS
 strawberry
 red currants
 raspberry

spices

MOUTHFEEL
Alcohol Heat

| 1 | | 5 | | | 10 |

Acidity Crispness

| 1 | | 5 | | | 10 |

Sugar Sweetness

| 1 | | 5 | | | 10 |

SERVE AT 🌡 46–50°F **COST** $

BEST TIME TO DRINK

| 1 year | 5 years | 10 year |

FOOD PAIRINGS
 aperitif
 charcuterie

 desserts with red fruit

YOU MIGHT ALSO LIKE
Cabernet d'Anjou, Rosé d'Anjou

WHITE WINES: CRISP AND FRUITY

Alsace Riesling
intense and elegant

ORIGIN: FRANCE
Alsace

VARIETALS
 riesling

COLOR

AROMAS
 white flowers citrus fruits white peach

minerality

MOUTHFEEL
Alcohol Heat

1	5	10

Acidity Crispness

1	5	10

SERVE AT 46-50°F **COST** $$

BEST TIME TO DRINK

1 year	5 years	10 years

FOOD PAIRINGS
 oysters crustaceans (small)

 grilled fish fish with sauce

sushi, raw fish white meat

YOU MIGHT ALSO LIKE
Alsace Grand Cru Riesling, Mosel-Saar-Ruwer (Germany)

Anjou
full-bodied and lively

ORIGIN: FRANCE
Loire Valley (Anjou and Saumur)

VARIETALS
chenin chardonnay

COLOR
 sauvignon

AROMAS
white flowers citrus fruits yellow peach

pear quince

MOUTHFEEL
Alcohol Heat

1	5	10

Acidity Crispness

1	5	10

SERVE AT 50-54°F **COST** $

BEST TIME TO DRINK

1 year	5 years	10 ye

FOOD PAIRINGS
 crustaceans (small) grilled fish

 quiches and savory tarts charcuterie

 white meat

YOU MIGHT ALSO LIKE
Saumur, Coteaux du Loir, Savennières

Also available in:
- late harvest Alsatian wine
- Alsace sélection de grains nobles

Also available in:
- red

Bergerac
aromatic and fresh

ORIGIN: FRANCE
Southwest

VARIETALS

 sauvignon sémillon muscadelle

COLOR

AROMAS

white flowers   citrus fruits   exotic fruit

almond   vanilla

MOUTHFEEL

Alcohol Heat

| 1 | 5 | 10 |

Acidity Crispness

| 1 | 5 | 10 |

SERVE AT 50-54°F **COST** $

BEST TIME TO DRINK

| 1 year | 5 years | 10 years |

FOOD PAIRINGS

 aperitif   crustaceans (small)

scallops   grilled fish

 fish with sauce   white meat

YOU MIGHT ALSO LIKE

White Bordeaux, Entre-Deux-Mers, Sauvignon Blanc (Côtes de Duras), Côtes du Marmandais, Sauvignon Blanc (Touraine), Pouilly-Fumé, Sancerre

Also available in:
● red
● rosé

White Bordeaux
fresh and aromatic

ORIGIN: FRANCE
Bordeaux

VARIETALS

sauvignon sémillon muscadelle

COLOR

AROMAS

white flowers   citrus fruits   exotic fruit

vanilla   almond

MOUTHFEEL

Alcohol Heat

| 1 | 5 | 10 |

Acidity Crispness

| 1 | 5 | 10 |

SERVE AT 50-54°F **COST** $

BEST TIME TO DRINK

| 1 year | 5 years | 10 years |

FOOD PAIRINGS

aperitif   oysters

 scallops   grilled fish

 fish with sauce   white meat

YOU MIGHT ALSO LIKE

Entre-Deux-Mers, Graves, Côtes de Bourg, Bergerac, Montravel, Buzet, Sancerre, Sauvignon Blanc (Touraine)

Also available in:
● red
● rosé

143

Chablis
lively, with minerality

ORIGIN: FRANCE
Burgundy (Chablis)

....

VARIETALS **COLOR**

 chardonnay

....

AROMAS

 white flowers   apple   citrus fruits

minerality   undergrowth

....

MOUTHFEEL

Alcohol Heat

1	5	10

Acidity Crispness

1	5	10

....

SERVE AT 50-54°F **COST** $$

BEST TIME TO DRINK

1 year	5 years	10 years

....

FOOD PAIRINGS

aperitif   oysters

sushi, raw fish   grilled fish

scallops   white meat

....

YOU MIGHT ALSO LIKE

Petit Chablis, Chablis Premier Cru, Chablis Grand Cru, Burgundy, Coteaux Champenois, Alsace Riesling

---

Chablis Grand Cru and Premier Cru
intense, with minerality

ORIGIN: FRANCE
Burgundy (Chablis)

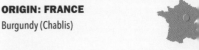

....

VARIETALS **COLOR**

 chardonnay

....

AROMAS

white flowers   citrus fruits   minerality

undergrowth   vanilla   butter

hazelnut   almond

....

MOUTHFEEL

Alcohol Heat

1	5	10

Acidity Crispness

1	5	10

....

SERVE AT 54-57°F **COST** $$ to $$$

BEST TIME TO DRINK

1 year	10 years	20 years

....

FOOD PAIRINGS

oysters   scallops

crustaceans (small) fish with sauce

white meat   poultry

....

YOU MIGHT ALSO LIKE

Chablis, Saint-Romain, Alsace Riesling Grand Cru

Chardonnay (Los Carneros)
structured and crisp

ORIGIN: UNITED STATES
North Coast of California
Napa Valley & Sonoma

VARIETALS **COLOR**
 chardonnay

AROMAS
citrus fruits | butter | vanilla
melon | almond | white flowers

MOUTHFEEL
Alcohol Heat

1	5	10

Acidity Crispness

1	5	10

SERVE AT 52-55°F **COST** $$$

BEST TIME TO DRINK

1 year	5 years	10 years

FOOD PAIRINGS
crustaceans (small) | goat milk cheese
grilled fish | scallops

YOU MIGHT ALSO LIKE
Saint-Véran, Mâcon-Villages, Chardonnay (Casablanca),
Chardonnay (Central Valley, Chile)

Chardonnay (Monterey)
supple and fresh

ORIGIN: UNITED STATES
Central Coast of California
Monterey County

VARIETALS **COLOR**
chardonnay

AROMAS
citrus fruits | exotic fruit | yellow peach
vanilla | toast

MOUTHFEEL
Alcohol Heat

1	5	10

Acidity Crispness

1	5	10

SERVE AT 52-55°F **COST** $ to $$$

BEST TIME TO DRINK

1 year	5 years	10 years

FOOD PAIRINGS
grilled fish | scallops
charcuterie | pressed cheese

YOU MIGHT ALSO LIKE
Saint-Véran, Meursault, Chablis Premier and
Grand Crus, Chardonnay (Casablanca)

Chardonnay (Russian River Valley)
crisp and elegant

ORIGIN: UNITED STATES
North Coast of California
Sonoma County

VARIETALS
chardonnay

COLOR

AROMAS
citrus fruits | butter | vanilla
yellow peach | almond | white flowers

MOUTHFEEL
Alcohol Heat

1	5	10

Acidity Crispness

1	5	10

SERVE AT 52-55°F **COST** $$ to $$$$$

BEST TIME TO DRINK

1 year	5 years	10 years

FOOD PAIRINGS
 grilled fish   crustaceans (small)
foie gras

YOU MIGHT ALSO LIKE
Saint-Véran, Pouilly-Fuissé, Chardonnay (Casablanca), Chardonnay (Central Valley, Chile)

Chardonnay (Sonoma Coast)
lively and fruity

ORIGIN: UNITED STATES
North Coast of California
Sonoma County

VARIETALS
chardonnay

COLOR

AROMAS
citrus fruits | butter | vanilla
yellow peach | hazelnut | white flowers

MOUTHFEEL
Alcohol Heat

1	5	10

Acidity Crispness

1	5	10

SERVE AT 52-55°F **COST** $$ to $$$$$

BEST TIME TO DRINK

1 year	5 years	10 years

FOOD PAIRINGS
 grilled fish   crustaceans (small)
pressed cheese

YOU MIGHT ALSO LIKE
Saint-Véran, Meursault, Chablis Premier and Grand Crus, Chardonnay (Casablanca)

Chardonnay (Willamette Valley)
structured and fragrant

ORIGIN: UNITED STATES
Oregon
Willamette Valley

VARIETALS
chardonnay

COLOR

AROMAS
citrus fruits   melon   yellow peach
butter   vanilla

MOUTHFEEL
Alcohol Heat

1	5	10

Acidity Crispness

1	5	10

SERVE AT 52-55°F   **COST** $$ to $$$$

BEST TIME TO DRINK

1 year	5 years	10 years

FOOD PAIRINGS
fish with sauce   crustaceans (small)
scallops   grilled fish

YOU MIGHT ALSO LIKE
Saint-Véran, Pouilly-Fuissé, Chardonnay (Casablanca), Chardonnay (Central Valley, Chile)

Chasselas (Fendant)
supple and light

ORIGIN: SWITZERLAND
Vaud and Valais

VARIETALS
chasselas

COLOR

AROMAS
white flowers   citrus fruits   minerality
hazelnut

MOUTHFEEL
Alcohol Heat

1	5	10

Acidity Crispness

1	5	10

SERVE AT 50-54°F   **COST** $$

BEST TIME TO DRINK

1 year	5 years	10 years

FOOD PAIRINGS
grilled fish   crustaceans (small)
pressed cheese   smoked fish

YOU MIGHT ALSO LIKE
Crépy, Pouilly-sur-Loire, Muscadet

Demi-Sec Chenin Blanc (South Africa)
decadent and fresh

ORIGIN: SOUTH AFRICA

VARIETALS

 chenin

COLOR

AROMAS

citrus fruits exotic fruit quince

apple

MOUTHFEEL

Alcohol Heat

1	5	10

Acidity Crispness

1	5	10

Sugar Sweetness

1	5	10

SERVE AT 46-50°F **COST** $ to $$

BEST TIME TO DRINK

1 year	5 years	10 years

FOOD PAIRINGS

 aperitif   yellow fruit desserts

YOU MIGHT ALSO LIKE

Vouvray, Montlouis-sur-Loire, Coteaux du Layon, Coteaux de l'Aubance

---

Entre-Deux-Mers
lively and aromatic

ORIGIN: FRANCE
Bordeaux (between the Garonne and Dordogne Rivers)

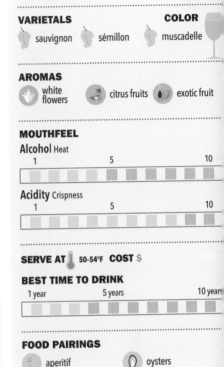

VARIETALS

sauvignon sémillon muscadelle

COLOR

AROMAS

white flowers citrus fruits exotic fruit

MOUTHFEEL

Alcohol Heat

1	5	10

Acidity Crispness

1	5	10

SERVE AT 50-54°F **COST** $

BEST TIME TO DRINK

1 year	5 years	10 years

FOOD PAIRINGS

aperitif oysters

crustaceans (small) grilled fish

fish with sauce white meat

YOU MIGHT ALSO LIKE

White Bordeaux, Bergerac Sec, Montravel, Sauvignon Blanc (Côtes de Duras), Buzet, Sauvignon Blanc (Touraine), Pouilly-Fumé, Sancerre

Frascati
supple and elegant

ORIGIN: ITALY
Lazio

VARIETALS

 malvasia bianca di candia

malvasia del lazio

COLOR

AROMAS

citrus fruits

white flowers

orange zest

white peach

green herbs

MOUTHFEEL
Alcohol Heat

1	5	10

Acidity Crispness

1	5	10

SERVE AT 46–50°F COST $ to $$

BEST TIME TO DRINK

1 year	5 years	10 years

FOOD PAIRINGS

aperitif

grilled fish

 crustaceans (small)

sushi, raw fish

 oysters

YOU MIGHT ALSO LIKE
Muscadet, Gros Plant du Pays Nantais, Trebbiano d'Abruzzo, Orvieto

---

Friulano Colli Orientali del Friuli
fragrant and intense

ORIGIN: ITALY
Friuli-Venezia Giulia

VARIETALS
friulano

COLOR

AROMAS

apple

almond

citrus fruits

green herbs

MOUTHFEEL
Alcohol Heat

1	5	10

Acidity Crispness

1	5	10

SERVE AT 46–50°F COST $$ to $$$

BEST TIME TO DRINK

1 year	5 years	10 years

FOOD PAIRINGS

shellfish

grilled fish

asparagus

smoked fish

YOU MIGHT ALSO LIKE
Sauvignon Blanc (Styria), Verdicchio dei Castelli di Jesi, Rueda

Fumé Blanc (Napa Valley)
complex and aromatic

ORIGIN: UNITED STATES
North Coast of California

VARIETALS
sauvignon blanc

COLOR

AROMAS

 citrus fruits   exotic fruit   green herbs

 white peach vanilla toast

MOUTHFEEL

Alcohol Heat

1	5	10

Acidity Crispness

1	5	10

SERVE AT 52-55°F **COST** $$ to $$$

BEST TIME TO DRINK

1 year	5 years	10 years

FOOD PAIRINGS

fish with sauce quiches and savory tarts

crustaceans (small) scallops

YOU MIGHT ALSO LIKE

White Passac-Léognan, Sauvignon Blanc, oaked (New Zealand), Sauvignon Blanc, oaked (South Africa), Sauvignon Blanc (Casablanca)

Gavi
lively and refreshing

ORIGIN: ITALY
Piedmont

VARIETALS
cortese

COLOR

AROMAS

 lemon apple green herbs

minerality white flowers grapefruit

MOUTHFEEL

Alcohol Heat

1	5	10

Acidity Crispness

1	5	10

SERVE AT 46-52°F **COST** $$ to $$$

BEST TIME TO DRINK

1 year	5 years	10 years

FOOD PAIRINGS

 aperitif   grilled fish

 crustaceans (small)   sushi, raw fish

YOU MIGHT ALSO LIKE

Verdicchio dei Castelli di Jesi, Ríais Baixas, Vinho Verde Entre-Deux-Mers

Greco di Tufo
fresh and structured

ORIGIN: ITALY
Campania

VARIETALS

 greco

 coda di volpe

COLOR

AROMAS

honey

white peach

apricot

exotic fruit

pear

MOUTHFEEL
Alcohol Heat

1	5	10

Acidity Crispness

1	5	10

SERVE AT 46–50°F **COST** $$ to $$$

BEST TIME TO DRINK

1 year	5 years	10 years

FOOD PAIRINGS

 poultry

grilled fish

crustaceans (small)

fish with sauce

smoked fish

YOU MIGHT ALSO LIKE
Condrieu, Viognier (Australia), Viognier (California)

Jurançon Sec
steely and fresh

ORIGIN: FRANCE
Southwest

VARIETALS

 gros manseng

 petit manseng

 COLOR

AROMAS

yellow peach

citrus fruits

exotic fruit

honey

MOUTHFEEL
Alcohol Heat

1	5	10

Acidity Crispness

1	5	10

SERVE AT 50–54°F **COST** $$

BEST TIME TO DRINK

1 year	5 years	10 years

FOOD PAIRINGS

 aperitif

 grilled fish

fish with sauce

white meat

YOU MIGHT ALSO LIKE
dry white Pacherenc du Vic Bilh, Irouléguy, Tursan

Muscadet Sèvre et Maine
vibrant, with minerality

ORIGIN: FRANCE
Loire Valley (Nantes)

VARIETALS
 Bourgogne

COLOR

AROMAS
 white flowers citrus fruits white peach
minerality

MOUTHFEEL
Alcohol Heat

1	5	10

Acidity Crispness

1	5	10

SERVE AT 46-50°F   **COST** $

BEST TIME TO DRINK

1 year	5 years	10 years

FOOD PAIRINGS

 oysters   shellfish

crustaceans (small)   sushi, raw fish

grilled fish   fish with sauce

YOU MIGHT ALSO LIKE
Muscadet (Nantes region), Gros Plant du Pays Nantais, Picpoul de Pinet, Alsace Sylvaner, Vinho Verde (Portugal)

Dry Muscat (Moscato) (California)
exuberant and fragrant

ORIGIN: UNITED STATES
California

VARIETALS
muscat

COLOR

AROMAS
yellow peach orange zest white flowers
rose   exotic fruit

MOUTHFEEL
Alcohol Heat

1	5	10

Acidity Crispness

1	5	10

SERVE AT 48-52°F   **COST** $ to $$$

BEST TIME TO DRINK

1 year	5 years	10 years

FOOD PAIRINGS

aperitif   Indian cuisine

 Chinese cuisine

YOU MIGHT ALSO LIKE
Alsace Muscat, Muscat sec (Langeudoc-Roussillon), Muscat (Hungary)

Orvieto
fresh and quaffable

ORIGIN: ITALY
Lazio and Umbria

VARIETALS

grechetto trebbiano

COLOR

AROMAS

lemon white flowers apple

anis

MOUTHFEEL
Alcohol Heat

1	5	10

Acidity Crispness

1	5	10

SERVE AT 46–50°F **COST** $ to $$

BEST TIME TO DRINK

1 year	5 years	10 years

FOOD PAIRINGS

 aperitif grilled fish

 shellfish smoked fish

YOU MIGHT ALSO LIKE

Muscadet, Gros Plant du Pays Nantais, Trebbiano d'Abruzzo, Entre-Deux-Mers, Petit Chablis

Pinot Grigio (Friuli Grave)
light and fresh

ORIGIN: ITALY
Friuli-Venezia Giulia

VARIETALS

pinot gris

COLOR

AROMAS

citrus fruits pear apple

white flowers

MOUTHFEEL
Alcohol Heat

1	5	10

Acidity Crispness

1	5	10

SERVE AT 45–48°F **COST** $ to $$

BEST TIME TO DRINK

1 year	5 years	10 years

FOOD PAIRINGS

aperitif   shellfish

 goat milk cheese   grilled fish

YOU MIGHT ALSO LIKE

Muscadet, Gros Plant du Pays Nantais, Trebbiano d'Abruzzo, Orvieto

Pinot Grigio
light and subtle

ORIGIN: ITALY
Trentino-Alto Adige, Friuli

....

VARIETALS   **COLOR**

 pinot gris

....

AROMAS

 citrus fruits   pear   apple

white flowers

....

MOUTHFEEL
Alcohol Heat

1	5	10

Acidity Crispness

1	5	10

....

SERVE AT 46-50°F   **COST** $ to $$

BEST TIME TO DRINK

1 year	5 years	10 years

....

FOOD PAIRINGS

 aperitif   grilled fish

 pressed cheese   shellfish

quiches and savory tarts

....

YOU MIGHT ALSO LIKE
Pinot Grigio (California, Australia), Chasselas

Pinot Grigio (California)
supple and soft

ORIGIN: UNITED STATES
California

....

VARIETALS   **COLOR**

pinot gris

....

AROMAS

apple   white flowers   exotic fruit

citrus fruits

....

MOUTHFEEL
Alcohol Heat

1	5	10

Acidity Crispness

1	5	10

....

SERVE AT 46-50°F   **COST** $ to $$

BEST TIME TO DRINK

1 year	5 years	10 years

....

FOOD PAIRINGS

 aperitif   pressed cheese

 quiches and savory tarts   grilled fish

....

YOU MIGHT ALSO LIKE
Pinot Grigio (Italy), Pinot Grigio (New Zealand)

Pinot Grigio (Willamette Valley)
easy-drinking and soft

ORIGIN: UNITED STATES
Oregon
Willamette Valley

VARIETALS
pinot gris

COLOR

AROMAS
- yellow peach
- exotic fruit
- orange
- citrus fruits
- apple
- white flowers

MOUTHFEEL

Alcohol Heat

| 1 | 5 | 10 |

Acidity Crispness

| 1 | 5 | 10 |

SERVE AT 48-54°F **COST** $ to $$

BEST TIME TO DRINK

| 1 year | 5 years | 10 years |

FOOD PAIRINGS
- aperitif
- grilled fish
- crustaceans (small)
- pressed cheese

YOU MIGHT ALSO LIKE
Pinot Gris

Pouilly-Fumé
firm and aromatic

ORIGIN: FRANCE
Central Loire Valley

VARIETALS
sauvignon (fumé blanc)

COLOR

AROMAS
- white flowers
- citrus fruits
- firewood
- minerality

MOUTHFEEL

Alcohol Heat

| 1 | 5 | 10 |

Acidity Crispness

| 1 | 5 | 10 |

SERVE AT 50-54°F **COST** $$

BEST TIME TO DRINK

| 1 year | 5 years | 10 years |

FOOD PAIRINGS
- aperitif
- oysters
- crustaceans (small)
- grilled fish
- fish with sauce
- smoked fish

YOU MIGHT ALSO LIKE
Sancerre, Quincy, Reuilly, Menetou-Salon, Coteaux du Giennois, Touraine Oisly, Sauvignon Blanc (Touraine), Bergerac Sec, Sauvignon Blanc (New Zealand), Sauvignon Blanc (Chile)

Rías Baixas
fresh and fragrant

ORIGIN: SPAIN
Galicia

VARIETALS

 albariño

COLOR

AROMAS

 apple   pear   citrus fruits

white flowers   white peach

MOUTHFEEL

Alcohol Heat

| 1 | 5 | 10 |

Acidity Crispness

| 1 | 5 | 10 |

SERVE AT 50-54°F   **COST** $$

BEST TIME TO DRINK

| 1 year | 5 years | 10 years |

FOOD PAIRINGS

 crustaceans (small)   goat milk cheese

 shellfish   grilled fish

 sushi, raw fish

YOU MIGHT ALSO LIKE

Vinho Verde (Portugal), Alvarinho, Rueda (Spain), Menetou-Salon, IGP Côtes de Gascogne, Sauvignon Blanc (Chile, South Africa, New Zealand)

Riesling (Wachau, Kremstal, Kamptal)
intense, with minerality

ORIGIN: AUSTRIA
Lower Austria

VARIETALS

 riesling

COLOR

AROMAS

 citrus fruits   yellow peach   minerality

smoked   white flowers

MOUTHFEEL

Alcohol Heat

| 1 | 5 | 10 |

Acidity Crispness

| 1 | 5 | 10 |

SERVE AT 46-50°F   **COST** $$ to $$$

BEST TIME TO DRINK

| 1 year | 5 years | 10 year |

FOOD PAIRINGS

 grilled fish   crustaceans (small)

 sushi, raw fish   oysters

smoked fish

YOU MIGHT ALSO LIKE

Riesling (Wachau), Alsace Riesling, Riesling (New Zealand)

Also available in:
 red

156

Riesling (Eden Valley)
firm and refined

ORIGIN: AUSTRALIA
South Australia

VARIETALS
riesling

COLOR

AROMAS

yellow peach   citronella   white flowers

citrus fruits   minerality   honey

smoked

MOUTHFEEL

Alcohol Heat

1	5	10

Acidity Crispness

1	5	10

SERVE AT 45-48°F   **COST** $$ to $$$

BEST TIME TO DRINK

1 year	10 years	20 years

FOOD PAIRINGS

sushi, raw fish   crustaceans (small)

smoked fish   shellfish

grilled fish

YOU MIGHT ALSO LIKE

Riesling (Wachau), Alsace Riesling, Riesling (New Zealand), Tokaj sec

---

Riesling (Clare Valley)
lively and aromatic

ORIGIN: AUSTRALIA
South Australia

VARIETALS
riesling

COLOR

AROMAS

yellow peach   citronella   white flowers

minerality   citrus fruits   smoked

honey

MOUTHFEEL

Alcohol Heat

1	5	10

Acidity Crispness

1	5	10

SERVE AT 45-48°F   **COST** $$ to $$$

BEST TIME TO DRINK

1 year	10 years	20 years

FOOD PAIRINGS

crustaceans (small)   sushi, raw fish

shellfish   grilled fish

pressed cheese

YOU MIGHT ALSO LIKE

Riesling (Wachau), Alsace Riesling, Riesling (New Zealand), Tokaj sec

Riesling
(Finger Lakes)
lively and aromatic

ORIGIN: UNITED STATES
New York

VARIETALS

riesling

COLOR

AROMAS

 citronella   citrus fruits   smoked

white flowers   apple   white peach

minerality

MOUTHFEEL

Alcohol Heat

1	5	10

Acidity Crispness

1	5	10

SERVE AT 50–54°F   **COST** $ to $$$

BEST TIME TO DRINK

1 year	10 years	20 years

FOOD PAIRINGS

goat milk cheese   crustaceans (small)

grilled fish   charcuterie

YOU MIGHT ALSO LIKE

Alsace Riesling, Riesling (Austria), Riesling (New Zealand), Riesling (Clare Valley)

Riesling
(New Zealand)
crisp and fruity

ORIGIN: NEW ZEALAND

VARIETALS

riesling

COLOR

AROMAS

citrus fruits   minerality   citronella

white flowers   yellow peach

MOUTHFEEL

Alcohol Heat

1	5	10

Acidity Crispness

1	5	10

SERVE AT 46–50°F   **COST** $$ to $$$$

BEST TIME TO DRINK

1 year	5 years	10 year

FOOD PAIRINGS

grilled fish   crustaceans (small)

oysters   goat milk cheese

YOU MIGHT ALSO LIKE

Alsace Riesling, Riesling (Austria), Riesling (Clare Valley)

Riesling (Washington)
nervy and clean

ORIGIN: UNITED STATES
Washington

VARIETALS
riesling

COLOR

AROMAS
citrus fruits · citronella · white flowers · white peach

MOUTHFEEL

Alcohol Heat

1	5	10

Acidity Crispness

1	5	10

SERVE AT 50-54°F **COST** $ to $$

BEST TIME TO DRINK

1 year	5 years	10 years

FOOD PAIRINGS
crustaceans (small) · grilled fish · charcuterie · oysters

YOU MIGHT ALSO LIKE
[Al]sace Riesling, Riesling (Austria), Riesling [N]ew Zealand), Riesling (Clare Valley)

Dry Riesling
lively and complex

ORIGIN: GERMANY
Mosel, Rheingau

VARIETALS
riesling

COLOR

AROMAS
citrus fruits · apple · white grape · white flowers · minerality

MOUTHFEEL

Alcohol Heat

1	5	10

Acidity Crispness

1	5	10

SERVE AT 46-50°F **COST** $$ to $$$

BEST TIME TO DRINK

1 year	5 years	10 years

FOOD PAIRINGS

 sushi, raw fish   oysters

 grilled fish scallops

YOU MIGHT ALSO LIKE
Alsace Riesling, Riesling (New Zealand), Riesling (Austria), Chablis, Cour Cheverny

Rueda
fruity and refreshing

ORIGIN: SPAIN
Castilla y León

VARIETALS
 verdejo

COLOR

AROMAS
 white flowers   citrus fruits   exotic fruit

green bell pepper

MOUTHFEEL
Alcohol Heat

1	5	10

Acidity Crispness

1	5	10

SERVE AT 50-54°F COST $$

BEST TIME TO DRINK

1 year	5 years	10 years

FOOD PAIRINGS
- crustaceans (small)
- charcuterie
- quiches and savory tarts
- goat milk cheese
- grilled fish

YOU MIGHT ALSO LIKE
Rías Baixas, Sauvignon Blanc (Chile), Sauvignon Blanc (California)

Also available in:
- red
- rosé

Sancerre
intense and aromatic

ORIGIN: FRANCE
Central Loire Valley

VARIETALS
sauvignon

COLOR

AROMAS
white flowers   citrus fruits   minerality

firewood

MOUTHFEEL
Alcohol Heat

1	5	10

Acidity Crispness

1	5	10

SERVE AT 50-54°F COST $$

BEST TIME TO DRINK

1 year	5 years	10 years

FOOD PAIRINGS
- aperitif
- crustaceans (small)
- fish with sauce
- oysters
- grilled fish
- sushi, raw fish

YOU MIGHT ALSO LIKE
Pouilly-Fumé, Reuilly, Menetou-Salon, Touraine Oisly, Sauvignon Blanc (Touraine), Entre-Deux-Mers, Bergerac Sec, White Bordeaux, Sauvignon Blanc (Côtes de Duras), Sauvignon Blanc (New Zealand), Sauvignon Blanc (Chile)

Also available in:
- red
- rosé

Sauvignon Blanc (Adelaide Hills)
refreshing and fragrant

ORIGIN: AUSTRALIA
South Australia

VARIETALS
 sauvignon blanc

COLOR

AROMAS
citrus fruits

 green herbs

white peach

firewood

white flowers

MOUTHFEEL
Alcohol Heat

1	5	10

Acidity Crispness

1	5	10

SERVE AT 48-52°F COST $$

BEST TIME TO DRINK

1 year	5 years	10 years

FOOD PAIRINGS
 goat milk cheese

grilled fish

 quiches and savory tarts

YOU MIGHT ALSO LIKE
Sancerre, Pouilly-Fumé, Sauvignon Blanc (Casablanca), Sauvignon Blanc (Constantia), Sauvignon Blanc (Styria)

Sauvignon Blanc (California)
fresh and fruity

ORIGIN: UNITED STATES
California

VARIETALS
sauvignon blanc

COLOR

AROMAS
citrus fruits   exotic fruit   green herbs

green bell pepper

MOUTHFEEL
Alcohol Heat

1	5	10

Acidity Crispness

1	5	10

SERVE AT 50-54°F COST $ to $$

BEST TIME TO DRINK

1 year	5 years	10 years

FOOD PAIRINGS
grilled fish   shellfish

 goat milk cheese   aperitif

YOU MIGHT ALSO LIKE
Sauvignon Blanc (Languedoc-Rouissillon), Entre-Deux-Mers, Sauvignon Blanc (Casablanca), Sauvignon Blanc (New Zealand)

Sauvignon Blanc (Casablanca Valley)
intense and fragrant

ORIGIN: CHILE

Casablanca Valley

VARIETALS

 sauvignon blanc

COLOR

AROMAS

citrus fruits

yellow peach

exotic fruit

green herbs

MOUTHFEEL

Alcohol Heat

1	5	10

Acidity Crispness

1	5	10

SERVE AT 46–50°F **COST** $$

BEST TIME TO DRINK

1 year	5 years	10 years

FOOD PAIRINGS

aperitif

grilled fish

quiches and savory tarts

YOU MIGHT ALSO LIKE

Sancerre, Pouilly-Fumé, Sauvignon Blanc (Casablanca), Sauvignon Blanc (Constantia), Sauvignon Blanc (Adelaide Hills)

Sauvignon Blanc (Constantia)
crisp and quaffable

ORIGIN: SOUTH AFRICA

Coastal Region

VARIETALS

sauvignon blanc

COLOR

AROMAS

citrus fruits

green herbs

 yellow peach

citronella

 firewood

MOUTHFEEL

Alcohol Heat

1	5	10

Acidity Crispness

1	5	10

SERVE AT 46–50°F **COST** $$

BEST TIME TO DRINK

1 year	5 years	10 year

FOOD PAIRINGS

grilled fish

sushi, raw fish

goat milk cheese

quiches and savory tarts

YOU MIGHT ALSO LIKE

Sancerre, Pouilly-Fumé, Sauvignon Blanc (Casablanca), Sauvignon Blanc (Adelaide Hills), Sauvignon Blanc (Styria)

Sauvignon Blanc (Marlborough)
lively and exuberant

ORIGIN: NEW ZEALAND
South Island Marlborough

VARIETALS **COLOR**
sauvignon blanc

AROMAS
citrus fruits   exotic fruit   green bell pepper

MOUTHFEEL

Alcohol Heat

1	5	10

Acidity Crispness

1	5	10

SERVE AT 50-54°F   **COST** $$$

BEST TIME TO DRINK

1 year	20 years	40 years

FOOD PAIRINGS

sushi, raw fish   crustaceans (small)

goat milk cheese   oysters

grilled fish

YOU MIGHT ALSO LIKE

Sauvignon Blanc (South Africa), Sauvignon Blanc (Chile), Sauvignon Blanc (Alto Adige, Italy), Sancerre, Pouilly-Fumé, Menetou-Salon, IGP Côtes de Gascogne

Sauvignon Blanc (Styria)
crisp and aromatic

ORIGIN: AUSTRIA
Styria

VARIETALS **COLOR**
sauvignon blanc

AROMAS
citrus fruits   white peach   green herbs

citronella   grapefruit

MOUTHFEEL

Alcohol Heat

1	5	10

Acidity Crispness

1	5	10

SERVE AT 46-50°F   **COST** $$ to $$$

BEST TIME TO DRINK

1 year	5 years	10 years

FOOD PAIRINGS

aperitif   crustaceans (small)

oysters   quiches and savory tarts

pressed cheese

YOU MIGHT ALSO LIKE

Sancerre, Pouilly-Fumé, Sauvignon Blanc (Casablanca), Sauvignon Blanc (Constantia), Sauvignon Blanc (Adelaide Hills)

Savoie Jacquère
light and quaffable

ORIGIN: FRANCE
Savoie and Bugey

VARIETALS   **COLOR**

 jacquère

AROMAS

 white flowers   citrus fruits   minerality

MOUTHFEEL
Alcohol Heat

1	5	10

Acidity Crispness

1	5	10

SERVE AT 46-50°F **COST** $

BEST TIME TO DRINK

1 year	5 years	10 years

FOOD PAIRINGS

grilled fish   crustaceans (small)

quiches and savory tarts   pressed cheese

YOU MIGHT ALSO LIKE

Alsace Sylvaner, Gros Plant du Pays Nantais,
Vinho Verde (Portugal)

Dry Tokaj
lively and clean

ORIGIN: HUNGARY
Tokaj

VARIETALS   **COLOR**

 furmint   hársevelü   sárga muskotály

AROMAS

 citrus fruits   minerality   smoked

white flowers   citronella   apple

quince

MOUTHFEEL
Alcohol Heat

1	5	10

Acidity Crispness

1	5	10

SERVE AT 50-52°F **COST** $$ to $$$

BEST TIME TO DRINK

1 year	5 years	10 years

FOOD PAIRINGS

 grilled fish   crustaceans (small)

 sushi, raw fish   oysters

YOU MIGHT ALSO LIKE

Chablis, Alsace Riesling, Riesling sec from Germany
(Mosel, Rheingau), Riesling (Wachau)

Touraine Sauvignon Blanc
lively and aromatic

ORIGIN: FRANCE

Loire Valley (Touraine)

VARIETALS   **COLOR**

 sauvignon

AROMAS

 white flowers   citrus fruits   minerality

firewood

MOUTHFEEL

Alcohol Heat

1	5	10

Acidity Crispness

1	5	10

SERVE AT 50–54°F   **COST** $

BEST TIME TO DRINK

1 year	5 years	10 years

FOOD PAIRINGS

aperitif   crustaceans (small)

grilled fish   fish with sauce

sushi, raw fish   asparagus

YOU MIGHT ALSO LIKE

Coteaux du Giennois, Sancerre, Pouilly-Fumé, Quincy, Menetou-Salon, Reuilly, White Bordeaux, Bergerac Sec

Trebbiano d'Abruzzo
lively and light

ORIGIN: ITALY

Abruzzo

VARIETALS   **COLOR**

trebbiano

AROMAS

citrus fruits   white flowers

MOUTHFEEL

Alcohol Heat

1	5	10

Acidity Crispness

1	5	10

SERVE AT 46–50°F   **COST** $ to $$

BEST TIME TO DRINK

1 year	5 years	10 years

FOOD PAIRINGS

aperitif   grilled fish

shellfish   smoked fish

YOU MIGHT ALSO LIKE

Muscadet, Gros Plant du Pays Nantais, Trebbiano d'Abruzzo, Entre-Deux-Mers, Petit Chablis

Verdicchio dei Castelli di Jesi
crisp and fragrant

ORIGIN: ITALY
Marches

VARIETALS   **COLOR**

 verdicchio

AROMAS

 citrus fruits   green herbs   almond

 white flowers

MOUTHFEEL
Alcohol Heat

| 1 | | 5 | | 10 |

Acidity Crispness

| 1 | | 5 | | 10 |

SERVE AT 🌡 48–52°F   **COST** $ to $$$

BEST TIME TO DRINK

| 1 year | 5 years | 10 years |

FOOD PAIRINGS

grilled fish   crustaceans (small)

shellfish   goat milk cheese

YOU MIGHT ALSO LIKE

Cortese di Gavi, Friulano from Colli Orientali del Friuli, Pouilly-Fumé, Rueda

Vinho Verde
vibrant and fruity

ORIGIN: PORTUGAL
Northern Porto, south of Galicia

VARIETALS   **COLOR**

alvarinho   arinto   avesso

azal   baroque   loureiro

trajadura

AROMAS

citrus fruits   apple   white flowers

exotic fruit

MOUTHFEEL
Alcohol Heat

| 1 | | 5 | | 10 |

Acidity Crispness

| 1 | | 5 | | 10 |

SERVE AT 🌡 46–50°F   **COST** $

BEST TIME TO DRINK

| 1 year | 5 years | 10 years |

FOOD PAIRINGS

 grilled fish   crustaceans (small)

 goat milk cheese   sushi, raw fish

YOU MIGHT ALSO LIKE

Rías Baixas, IGP Côtes de Gascogne, Entre-Deux-Mers, Picpoul de Pinet, Muscadet Sèvre et Maine

Also available in:
 red
rosé

WHITE WINES: FULL AND ROUND

Alsace Gewürztraminer
unctuous and aromatic

ORIGIN: FRANCE
Alsace

VARIETALS

 Gewürztraminer

COLOR

AROMAS

 rose   exotic fruit black pepper

MOUTHFEEL

Alcohol Heat

1	5	10

Acidity Crispness

1	5	10

Sugar Sweetness

1	5	10

SERVE AT 50-54°F **COST** $$

BEST TIME TO DRINK

1 year	5 years	10 years

FOOD PAIRINGS

aperitif foie gras

poultry Chinese cuisine

washed rind cheese yellow fruit dessert

YOU MIGHT ALSO LIKE

German Gewürztraminer, IGP Côtes de Gascogne, Côtes du Rhône Viognier

---

Alsace Pinot Gris
round and full-bodied

ORIGIN: FRANCE
Alsace

VARIETALS

 pinot gris

COLOR

AROMAS

yellow peach   citrus fruits honey

 undergrowth

MOUTHFEEL

Alcohol Heat

1	5	10

Acidity Crispness

1	5	10

Sugar Sweetness

1	5	10

SERVE AT 50-54°F **COST** $$

BEST TIME TO DRINK

1 year	5 years	10 years

FOOD PAIRINGS

 white meat   poultry

quiches and savory tarts   fish with sauce

 washed rind cheese

YOU MIGHT ALSO LIKE

Coteaux d'Ancenis Malvoisie

Also available in:
- Vendanges tardives
- Sélection de grains nobles

Also available in:
- Vendanges tardives
- Sélection de grains nobles

Assyrtiko (Santorini)
intense, with minerality

ORIGIN: GREECE
Santorini

VARIETALS

 assyrtiko

COLOR

AROMAS

citrus fruits   minerality   yellow peach

apricot

MOUTHFEEL

Alcohol Heat

1			5			10

Acidity Crispness

1			5			10

SERVE AT 50-54°F   **COST** $$ to $$$$

BEST TIME TO DRINK

1 year		5 years		10 years

FOOD PAIRINGS

grilled fish   crustaceans (small)

fish with sauce   scallops

YOU MIGHT ALSO LIKE

Fiano di Avellino, Grüner Veltliner (Wachau),
White Châteauneuf-du-Pape, Chablis Grand Cru,
Alsace Riesling

Burgundy
supple and refined

ORIGIN: FRANCE
Burgundy (regional appellations)

VARIETALS

chardonnay

COLOR

AROMAS

white flowers   citrus fruits   butter

almond   hazelnut   toast

MOUTHFEEL

Alcohol Heat

1			5			10

Acidity Crispness

1			5			10

SERVE AT 50-54°F   **COST** $

BEST TIME TO DRINK

1 year		5 years		10 years

FOOD PAIRINGS

aperitif   crustaceans (small)

scallops   grilled fish

 fish with sauce   white meat

YOU MIGHT ALSO LIKE

Chablis, Saint-Romain, Montagny, Mâcon-Villages,
Saint-Véran

Also available in:
- red
- rosé

Chardonnay (Australia)
soft and opulent

ORIGIN: AUSTRALIA

VARIETALS

chardonnay

COLOR

AROMAS

- yellow peach
- exotic fruit
- honey
- vanilla
- toast

MOUTHFEEL

Alcohol Heat

1	5	10

Acidity Crispness

1	5	10

SERVE AT 50-54°F **COST** $$ to $$$

BEST TIME TO DRINK

1 year	5 years	10 years

FOOD PAIRINGS

- white meat
- fish with sauce
- quiches and savory tarts
- scallops

YOU MIGHT ALSO LIKE

Pouilly-Fuissé, Saint-Véran, IGP Pays d'Oc Chardonnay, Chardonnay (California, Chile, Argentina)

Chardonnay (Adelaide Hills)
fresh and structured

ORIGIN: AUSTRALIA
South Australia

VARIETALS

chardonnay

COLOR

AROMAS

- vanilla
- citrus fruits
- yellow peach
- butter
- toast
- melon
- white flowers

MOUTHFEEL

Alcohol Heat

1	5	10

Acidity Crispness

1	5	10

SERVE AT 48-52°F **COST** $$ to $$$

BEST TIME TO DRINK

1 year	5 years	10 year

FOOD PAIRINGS

 fish with sauce
 pressed cheese
 white meat
 scallops
 crustaceans (small)

YOU MIGHT ALSO LIKE

Chardonnay (Casablanca), Saint-Véran, Mâcon-Village Chardonnay (Monterrey), Chardonnay (Russian River Valley)

Chardonnay (California)
round and exotic

ORIGIN: UNITED STATES
California

VARIETALS

 chardonnay

COLOR

AROMAS

yellow peach

exotic fruit

citrus fruits

vanilla

melon

butter

MOUTHFEEL

Alcohol Heat

1				5					10

Acidity Crispness

1				5					10

SERVE AT 50-54°F **COST** $ to $$

BEST TIME TO DRINK

1 year			5 years					10 years

FOOD PAIRINGS

pressed cheese

quiches and savory tarts

grilled fish

aperitif

YOU MIGHT ALSO LIKE

Chardonnay (Sicily), Chardonnay (Chile), Chardonnay (Languedoc-Rouissillon), Chardonnay (Australia), Chardonnay (South Africa)

Chardonnay (Casablanca Valley)
aromatic and fresh

ORIGIN: CHILE
Casablanca Valley

VARIETALS

chardonnay

COLOR

AROMAS

citrus fruits

melon

white flowers

vanilla

exotic fruit

butter

MOUTHFEEL

Alcohol Heat

1				5					10

Acidity Crispness

1				5					10

SERVE AT 48-54°F **COST** $$

BEST TIME TO DRINK

1 year			5 years					10 years

FOOD PAIRINGS

aperitif

grilled fish

scallops

pressed cheese

quiches and savory tarts

YOU MIGHT ALSO LIKE

Chardonnay (Adelaide Hills), Saint-Véran, Mâcon-Villages, Chardonnay (Monterrey), Chardonnay (Russian River Valley)

Chardonnay (Central Valley)
smooth and round

ORIGIN: CHILE
Central Valley

VARIETALS

chardonnay

COLOR

AROMAS

yellow peach

melon

vanilla

mango

pineapple

butter

toast

MOUTHFEEL

Alcohol Heat

1	5	10

Acidity Crispness

1	5	10

SERVE AT 50-54°F **COST** $ to $$

BEST TIME TO DRINK

1 year	5 years	10 years

FOOD PAIRINGS

white meat

fish with sauce

scallops

pressed cheese

quiches and savory tarts

YOU MIGHT ALSO LIKE

Chardonnay (Sicily), Chardonnay (Pays d'Oc), Mâcon-Villages, Chardonnay (Mendoza), Chardonnay (California)

Chardonnay (Margaret River)
intense and fleshy

ORIGIN: AUSTRALIA
Western Australia

VARIETALS

chardonnay

COLOR

AROMAS

yellow peach

vanilla

citrus fruit

butter

brioche

exotic fruit

MOUTHFEEL

Alcohol Heat

1	5	10

Acidity Crispness

1	5	10

SERVE AT 50-54°F **COST** $$ to $$$$

BEST TIME TO DRINK

1 year	10 years	20 years

FOOD PAIRINGS

white meat

fish with sauce

pressed cheese

scallops

YOU MIGHT ALSO LIKE

Meursault, Pouilly-Fuissé, Chardonnay (Napa Valley), Chardonnay (Mendoza)

Chardonnay (Marlborough)
structured and intense

ORIGIN: NEW ZEALAND
uth Island

VARIETALS

 chardonnay

COLOR

AROMAS

 citrus fruits vanilla toast

white flowers yellow peach exotic fruit

MOUTHFEEL

Alcohol Heat

1	5	10

Acidity Crispness

1	5	10

SERVE AT 50-55°F **COST** $$ to $$$$

BEST TIME TO DRINK

year	5 years	10 years

FOOD PAIRINGS

 crustaceans (small) white meat

mushrooms fish with sauce

pressed cheese

YOU MIGHT ALSO LIKE

ardonnay (Casablanca), Saint-Véran, Mâcon-Villages, ardonnay (Monterrey), Chardonnay (Adelaide Hills)

Chardonnay (Mendoza)
powerful and fleshy

ORIGIN: ARGENTINA
Mendoza

VARIETALS

 chardonnay

COLOR

AROMAS

 yellow peach   mango   butter

 vanilla   pineapple   exotic fruit

MOUTHFEEL

Alcohol Heat

1	5	10

Acidity Crispness

1	5	10

SERVE AT 48-54°F **COST** $ to $$$

BEST TIME TO DRINK

1 year	5 years	10 years

FOOD PAIRINGS

 fish with sauce   pressed cheese

quiches and savory tarts

YOU MIGHT ALSO LIKE

Chardonnay (Chile), Pouilly-Fuissé, Chardonnay (Napa Valley), Chardonnay (Sicily)

Chardonnay (Santa Cruz Mountains)
elegant and complex

ORIGIN: UNITED STATES

Central Coast of California
Santa Cruz Mountains

VARIETALS   **COLOR**
 chardonnay

AROMAS
 citrus fruits   yellow peach   exotic fruit
butter   vanilla   hazelnut

MOUTHFEEL
Alcohol Heat

1	5	10

Acidity Crispness

1	5	10

SERVE AT 52-55°F   **COST** $$$ to $$$$$

BEST TIME TO DRINK

1 year	5 years	10 years

FOOD PAIRINGS
grilled fish   foie gras
poultry   fish with sauce

YOU MIGHT ALSO LIKE
Saint-Véran, Pouilly-Fuissé, Chardonnay (Casablanca), Chardonnay (Central Valley, Chile)

Chardonnay (Sicily)
supple and round

ORIGIN: ITALY
Sicily

VARIETALS   **COLOR**
 chardonnay

AROMAS
pineapple   butter   vanilla
yellow peach   toast

MOUTHFEEL
Alcohol Heat

1	5	10

Acidity Crispness

1	5	10

SERVE AT 48-54°F   **COST** $ to $$

BEST TIME TO DRINK

1 year	5 years	10 years

FOOD PAIRINGS
scallops   fish with sauce
quiches and savory tarts   poultry

YOU MIGHT ALSO LIKE
Chardonnay (Sicily), Chardonnay (Chile), Chardonnay (Languedoc-Rouissillon), Chardonnay (Australia), Chardonnay (South Africa)

Chardonnay (Sonoma)
round and fragrant

ORIGIN: UNITED STATES
California (Sonoma Valley)

VARIETALS
chardonnay

COLOR

AROMAS

yellow peach — citrus fruits — exotic fruit

spices — vanilla

MOUTHFEEL

Alcohol Heat
| 1 | 5 | 10 |

Acidity Crispness
| 1 | 5 | 10 |

SERVE AT 50-54°F **COST** $$ to $$$

BEST TIME TO DRINK
| 1 year | 5 years | 10 years |

FOOD PAIRINGS

white meat — crustaceans (small)

fish with sauce — scallops

YOU MIGHT ALSO LIKE
Pouilly-Fuissé, IGP Pays d'Oc Chardonnay, Chardonnay (Australia, Argentina, South Africa)

Chardonnay (Walker Bay)
complex and balanced

ORIGIN: SOUTH AFRICA
Cape South Coast

VARIETALS
chardonnay

COLOR

AROMAS

yellow peach — citrus fruits — butter

vanilla — white flowers — exotic fruit

MOUTHFEEL

Alcohol Heat
| 1 | 5 | 10 |

Acidity Crispness
| 1 | 5 | 10 |

SERVE AT 50-54°F **COST** $$ to $$$$

BEST TIME TO DRINK
| 1 year | 5 years | 10 years |

FOOD PAIRINGS

white meat — fish with sauce

pressed cheese

YOU MIGHT ALSO LIKE
Chardonnay (Casablanca), Saint-Véran, Mâcon-Villages, Chardonnay (Monterrey), Chardonnay (Russian River Valley)

Chassagne-Montrachet
round and viscous

ORIGIN: FRANCE
Burgundy (Côte de Beaune)

VARIETALS
 chardonnay

COLOR

AROMAS
white flowers | pear | citrus fruits

butter | honey | toast

MOUTHFEEL
Alcohol Heat

1	5	10

Acidity Crispness

1	5	10

SERVE AT 54-57°F COST $$$

BEST TIME TO DRINK

1 year	5 years	10 years

FOOD PAIRINGS
 fish with sauce | scallops

white meat | poultry

pressed cheese | crustaceans (small)

YOU MIGHT ALSO LIKE
Montrachet, Puligny-Montrachet, Meursault, Saint-Aubin, Corton-Charlemagne, Pouilly-Fuissé

Chenin Blanc (South Africa)
refreshing and crisp

ORIGIN: SOUTH AFRICA

VARIETALS
 chenin

COLOR

AROMAS
 citrus fruits | white flowers | exotic fruit

toast | vanilla

MOUTHFEEL
Alcohol Heat

1	5	10

Acidity Crispness

1	5	10

SERVE AT 50-54°F COST $$

BEST TIME TO DRINK

1 year	5 years	10 yea

FOOD PAIRINGS
 grilled fish | pressed cheese

white meat | fish with sauce

YOU MIGHT ALSO LIKE
Vouvray, Montlouis-sur-Loire, Saumur, Anjou

Also available in:
● red

Condrieu
round and floral

ORIGIN: FRANCE
Northern Rhone Valley

VARIETALS

 viognier

COLOR

AROMAS

 yellow peach

apricot

 violet

honey

white flowers

MOUTHFEEL

Alcohol Heat

1				5					10

Acidity Crispness

1				5					10

SERVE AT 54-57°F **COST** $$$ to $$$$

BEST TIME TO DRINK

1 year		5 years				10 years

FOOD PAIRINGS

 fish with sauce

scallops

 white meat

Middle Eastern cuisine

Chinese cuisine

YOU MIGHT ALSO LIKE

Château-Grillet, Côtes du Rhône Viognier, IGP Ardèche Viognier, New World Viognier

Corsica or Vin-de-Corse
full-bodied and aromatic

ORIGIN: FRANCE
Corsica

VARIETALS

 vermentino

COLOR

AROMAS

 white flowers

citrus fruits

 exotic fruit

MOUTHFEEL

Alcohol Heat

1				5					10

Acidity Crispness

1				5					10

SERVE AT 50-54°F **COST** $$

BEST TIME TO DRINK

1 year		5 years				10 years

FOOD PAIRINGS

 aperitif

 fish with sauce

goat milk cheese

 crustaceans (small)

 grilled fish

YOU MIGHT ALSO LIKE

Ajaccio, Patrimonio, Côtes du Roussillon

Also available in:
● red
● rosé

Corton-Charlemagne
majestic and refined

ORIGIN: FRANCE
Burgundy (Côte de Beaune)

VARIETALS
 chardonnay

COLOR

AROMAS
 white flowers
 citrus fruits
 exotic fruit

 minerality
 vanilla
almond

honey
truffle
butter

MOUTHFEEL
Alcohol Heat

1				5				10

Acidity Crispness

1				5				10

SERVE AT 54-57°F **COST** $$$$$

BEST TIME TO DRINK

1 year	5 years	10 years	15 years	20 years

FOOD PAIRINGS
 fish with sauce
 scallops

 crustaceans (small)
 poultry

white meat

YOU MIGHT ALSO LIKE
Montrachet, Puligny-Montrachet, Chassagne-Montrachet, Meursault, Saint-Aubin, Pouilly-Fuissé

Fiano di Avellino
versatile with minerality

ORIGIN: ITALY
Campania

VARIETALS
 fiano

COLOR

AROMAS
yellow peach
apricot
melon

mango
hazelnut
honey

MOUTHFEEL
Alcohol Heat

1				5				10

Acidity Crispness

1				5				10

SERVE AT 48-52°F **COST** $$ to $$$

BEST TIME TO DRINK

1 year	5 years	10 years

FOOD PAIRINGS
 fish with sauce
 scallops

 crustaceans (small)
mushroom

YOU MIGHT ALSO LIKE
Grüner Veltliner (Wachau), White Châteauneuf-du-Pape, Condrieu, Viognier (California)

Gerwürtztraminer (Anderson Valley)

soft and aromatic

ORIGIN: UNITED STATES
North Coast of California
Mendocino County

VARIETALS
 Gewürtztraminer

COLOR

AROMAS
 exotic fruit — rose — cinnamon

ginger

MOUTHFEEL

Alcohol Heat

1				5					10

Acidity Crispness

1				5					10

SERVE AT 48-54°F **COST** $$ to $$$

BEST TIME TO DRINK

1 year				5 years					10 years

FOOD PAIRINGS

aperitif — Indian cuisine

foie gras — poultry

YOU MIGHT ALSO LIKE
Alace Gewürztraminer

Graves
crisp and aromatic

ORIGIN: FRANCE
Bordeaux (Graves)

VARIETALS
 sauvignon — sémillon — muscadelle

COLOR

AROMAS
 white flowers — citrus fruits — white peach

exotic fruit — vanilla

MOUTHFEEL

Alcohol Heat

1				5					10

Acidity Crispness

1				5					10

SERVE AT 54-57°F **COST** $$

BEST TIME TO DRINK

1 year				5 years					10 years

FOOD PAIRINGS

 oysters — crustaceans (small)

 grilled fish — fish with sauce

white meat

YOU MIGHT ALSO LIKE
Passac-Léognan, White Bordeaux, Côtes de Bourg

Also available in:
● rouge

Grüner Veltliner (Wachau)
structured and complex

ORIGIN: AUSTRIA
Wachau

VARIETALS

 grüner veltliner

COLOR

AROMAS

 citrus fruits · white grape · black pepper

minerality · honey · toast

MOUTHFEEL

Alcohol Heat

1				5					10

Acidity Crispness

1				5					10

SERVE AT 50-54°F **COST** $$ to $$$$

BEST TIME TO DRINK

1 year	5 years	10 years	15 years	20 years

FOOD PAIRINGS

crustaceans (small) · white meat

fish with sauce · foie gras

YOU MIGHT ALSO LIKE

other Grüner Veltliner (Austria), Saumur, Savennières, Vouvray Sec, Chablis

---

Languedoc-Roussillon
flavorful and fresh

ORIGIN: FRANCE
Languedoc-Roussillon

VARIETALS

 cabernet sauvignon · clairette

 marsanne · piquepoul

vermentino

COLOR

 grenache blanc

 roussanne

AROMAS

citrus fruits · apricot · scrubland

 honey

MOUTHFEEL

Alcohol Heat

1				5					10

Acidity Crispness

1				5					10

SERVE AT 54-57°F **COST** $$

BEST TIME TO DRINK

1 year	5 years	10 years

FOOD PAIRINGS

grilled fish · fish with sauce

white meat · poultry

 goat milk cheese

YOU MIGHT ALSO LIKE

Corbières, Faugères, Saint-Chinian, Minervois, Côtes du Roussillon

Also available in:
● red
● rosé

Limoux
intense and oaky

ORIGIN: FRANCE
Languedoc-Roussillon

VARIETALS **COLOR**

chardonnay

AROMAS

white flowers

white peach

hazelnut

vanilla

scrubland

toast

MOUTHFEEL

Alcohol Heat

1	5	10

Acidity Crispness

1	5	10

SERVE AT 50-54°F **COST** $

BEST TIME TO DRINK

1 year	5 years	10 years

FOOD PAIRINGS

 fish with sauce

 white meat

poultry

goat milk cheese

YOU MIGHT ALSO LIKE

Meursault, Pouilly-Fuissé, Saint-Véran, IGP Ardèche Chardonnay, New World Chardonnay

---

Mâcon-Villages
expressive and balanced

ORIGIN: FRANCE
Burgundy (Mâcon)

VARIETALS **COLOR**

chardonnay

AROMAS

white flowers

white peach

citrus fruits

exotic fruit

vanilla

MOUTHFEEL

Alcohol Heat

1	5	10

Acidity Crispness

1	5	10

SERVE AT 50-54°F **COST** $

BEST TIME TO DRINK

1 year	5 years	10 years

FOOD PAIRINGS

aperitif

 crustaceans (small)

charcuterie

 quiches and savory tarts

poultry

white meat

YOU MIGHT ALSO LIKE

Saint-Véran, Viré-Clessé, Pouilly-Fuissé, Montagny, Beaujolais, Limoux, IGP Ardèche

---

Also available in:
red

181

Meursault
round and opulent

ORIGIN: FRANCE
Burgundy (Mâcon)

VARIETALS

 chardonnay

COLOR

AROMAS

 white flowers
 citrus fruits
exotic fruit

apricot
butter
hazelnut

toast

MOUTHFEEL

Alcohol Heat

| 1 | | | | 5 | | | | | 10 |

Acidity Crispness

| 1 | | | | 5 | | | | | 10 |

SERVE AT 54-57°F **COST** $$$

BEST TIME TO DRINK

| 1 year | 5 years | 10 years | 15 years | 20 years |

FOOD PAIRINGS

 fish with sauce
 crustaceans (small)

scallops
foie gras

poultry
white meat

YOU MIGHT ALSO LIKE

Montrachet, Puligny-Montrachet, Chassagne-Montrachet, Corton-Charlemagne, Saint-Aubin, Pouilly-Fuissé

Montrachet and Montrachet Grand Crus
unctuous with excellent depth

ORIGIN: FRANCE
Burgundy (Côtes de Beaune)

VARIETALS

 chardonnay

COLOR

AROMAS

white flowers
citrus fruits
butter

hazelnut
almond
minerality

cinnamon
honey

MOUTHFEEL

Alcohol Heat

| 1 | | | | 5 | | | | | 10 |

Acidity Crispness

| 1 | | | | 5 | | | | | 10 |

SERVE AT 54-57°F **COST** $$$$$

BEST TIME TO DRINK

| 1 year | 5 years | 10 years | 15 years | 20 years |

FOOD PAIRINGS

 fish with sauce
 crustaceans (small)

 scallops
 poultry

 white meat

YOU MIGHT ALSO LIKE

Corton-Charlemagne, Meursault, Saint-Aubin, Puligny-Montrachet, Chassagne-Montrachet, Pouilly-Fuissé, New World Chardonnay

---

Also available in:
 red

Pessac-Léognan
concentrated and complex

ORIGIN: FRANCE
Bordeaux (Graves)

VARIETALS
sauvignon   sémillon   muscadelle

COLOR

AROMAS
white flowers   citrus fruits   exotic fruit

hazelnut   toast

MOUTHFEEL

Alcohol Heat

1	5	10

Acidity Crispness

1	5	10

SERVE AT 50–54°F   **COST** $$$ to $$$$

BEST TIME TO DRINK

1 year	5 years	10 years

FOOD PAIRINGS
fish with sauce   scallops

crustaceans (small)   white meat

poultry   pressed cheese

YOU MIGHT ALSO LIKE
Graves, barrel-aged Bordeaux and Bergerac blancs

Pinot Grigio (Colli Orientali del Friuli)
intense and concentrated

ORIGIN: ITALY
Friuli-Venezia Giulia

VARIETALS
pinot gris

COLOR

AROMAS
exotic fruit   yellow peach   white flowers

apricot   citrus fruits

MOUTHFEEL

Alcohol Heat

1	5	10

Acidity Crispness

1	5	10

SERVE AT 46–52°F   **COST** $$ to $$$

BEST TIME TO DRINK

1 year	5 years	10 years

FOOD PAIRINGS
shellfish   fish with sauce

quiches and savory tarts   crustaceans (small)

YOU MIGHT ALSO LIKE
Alsace Pinot Gris, Pinot Grigio (New Zealand)

Also available in:
● red

Pouilly-Fuissé
steely and rich

ORIGIN: FRANCE
Burgundy (Mâcon)

VARIETALS **COLOR**

 chardonnay

AROMAS

white flowers | butter | honey

hazelnut | citrus fruits

MOUTHFEEL

Alcohol Heat
1   5   10

Acidity Crispness
1   5   10

SERVE AT 54-57°F **COST** $$

BEST TIME TO DRINK
1 year   5 years   10 years

FOOD PAIRINGS

fish with sauce | crustaceans (small)

scallops | poultry

white meat

YOU MIGHT ALSO LIKE

Pouilly-Loché, Pouilly-Vinzelles, Meursault, Puligny-Montrachet, Chassagne-Montrachet, Saint-Véran, Limoux, Chardonnay (California)

Puligny-Montrachet
dense and complex

ORIGIN: FRANCE
Burgundy (Côtes de Beaune)

VARIETALS **COLOR**

chardonnay

AROMAS

white flowers | citrus fruits | apple

almond | hazelnut | butter

minerality

MOUTHFEEL

Alcohol Heat
1   5   10

Acidity Crispness
1   5   10

SERVE AT 54-57°F **COST** $$$

BEST TIME TO DRINK
1 year   5 years   10 years   15 years   20 years

FOOD PAIRINGS

fish with sauce | scallops

crustaceans (small) | poultry

white meat

YOU MIGHT ALSO LIKE

Montrachet, Chassagne-Montrachet, Meursault, Saint-Aubin, Beaune, Corton-Charlemagne

Also available in:
● red (rare)

Sémillon (Hunter Valley)
smokey with minerality

ORIGIN: AUSTRALIA
New South Wales

VARIETALS   **COLOR**

🍇 sémillon

AROMAS

🔵 minerality   〰️ smoked   ⬤ honey

MOUTHFEEL

Alcohol Heat

1				5				10

Acidity Crispness

1				5				10

SERVE AT 🌡 50–54°F   **COST** $ to $$$

BEST TIME TO DRINK

1 year		10 years			20 years

FOOD PAIRINGS

🐟 grilled fish   🥧 quiches and savory tarts

🦪 oysters

YOU MIGHT ALSO LIKE

Vintage Riesling, Tokaj sec, Oloroso Sherry, Assyrtiko (Santorini)

Soave
soft and fresh

ORIGIN: ITALY
Veneto

VARIETALS   **COLOR**

🍇 garganega

AROMAS

⬇️ white flowers   🍐 pear   🍎 apple

⬤ white pepper

MOUTHFEEL

Alcohol Heat

1				5				10

Acidity Crispness

1				5				10

SERVE AT 🌡 54–57°F   **COST** $ to $$

BEST TIME TO DRINK

1 year		5 years			10 years

FOOD PAIRINGS

🐟 grilled fish   🦪 scallops

🧀 pressed cheese

YOU MIGHT ALSO LIKE

Saint-Joseph, Côtes du Rhône, Corsican Wine

Torrontès (Salta)
soft and aromatic

Vin Jaune
full-bodied and spicy

ORIGIN: ARGENTINA
Salta

ORIGIN: FRANCE
Jura

VARIETALS **COLOR**

 Torrontès

VARIETALS **COLOR**

savagnin

AROMAS

 white grape   yellow peach   white flowers

exotic fruit   raisin   orange zest

AROMAS

apple   citrus fruits   walnut

hazelnut   almond

MOUTHFEEL
Alcohol Heat

1	5	10

Acidity Crispness

1	5	10

MOUTHFEEL
Alcohol Heat

1	5	10

Acidity Crispness

1	5	10

SERVE AT 46–50°F **COST** $ to $$

BEST TIME TO DRINK

1 year	5 years	10 years

SERVE AT 54–57°F **COST** $$$

BEST TIME TO DRINK

1 year	10 years	20 years	30 years	40 years	50 years

FOOD PAIRINGS

 asparagus   aperitif

 Middle Eastern cuisine   Chinese cuisine

FOOD PAIRINGS

 crustaceans (small)   poultry

 white meat   fish with sauce

 pressed cheese

YOU MIGHT ALSO LIKE

Muscat sec, Sauvignon Blanc (Marlborough), Entre-Deux-Mers

YOU MIGHT ALSO LIKE

Savagnin Côtes du Jura Tradition, Sherry Fino

Viognier (California)
viscous and fragrant

ORIGIN: UNITED STATES
California

VARIETALS   **COLOR**

 viognier

AROMAS

 yellow peach   apricot   violet

vanilla   peony

MOUTHFEEL

Alcohol Heat

1	5	10

Acidity Crispness

1	5	10

SERVE AT 52-55°F **COST** $ to $$$$$

BEST TIME TO DRINK

1 year	5 years	10 years

FOOD PAIRINGS

aperitif   foie gras

scallops

YOU MIGHT ALSO LIKE

Condrieu, Viognier (Australia), Viognier (Languedoc-Rouissillon)

Viognier (Oregon)
round and smooth

ORIGIN: UNITED STATES
Oregon

VARIETALS   **COLOR**

viognier

AROMAS

yellow peach   apricot   violet

honey   vanilla

MOUTHFEEL

Alcohol Heat

1	5	10

Acidity Crispness

1	5	10

SERVE AT 52-55°F **COST** $$ to $$$

BEST TIME TO DRINK

1 year	5 years	10 years

FOOD PAIRINGS

aperitif   foie gras

Indian cuisine   poultry

scallops

YOU MIGHT ALSO LIKE

Condrieu, Viognier (Australia), Viognier (Languedoc-Rouissillon)

Sherry Fino
powerful and atypical

ORIGIN: SPAIN
Andalusia

VARIETALS

 palomino

COLOR

AROMAS

 apple   hazelnut   almond

spices

MOUTHFEEL

Alcohol Heat

1	5	10

Acidity Crispness

1	5	10

SERVE AT 54–57°F **COST** $$

BEST TIME TO DRINK

1 year	5 years	10 years

FOOD PAIRINGS

 aperitif   charcuterie

shellfish

YOU MIGHT ALSO LIKE

Manzanilla, Jura wine made with Savagnin (Château-Chalon, Côtes du Jura, L'Étoile, Arbois)

Sherry Oloroso
maderized and decadent

ORIGIN: SPAIN
Andalusia

VARIETALS

 palomino

COLOR

AROMAS

coffee   dried fruit   cinnamon

walnut   leather   caramel

MOUTHFEEL

Alcohol Heat

1	5	10

Acidity Crispness

1	5	10

SERVE AT 50–55°F **COST** $$ to $$$

BEST TIME TO DRINK

1 year	5 years	10 years

FOOD PAIRINGS

 aperitif   blue cheese

furred game   smoked fish

washed rind cheese

YOU MIGHT ALSO LIKE

Madère (dry), Tawny Port, Marsala (dry), Banyuls Grand Cru, Maury Tuilé, Rivesaltes Hors d'Âge

Also available in:
○ white
● rosé

WHITE WINES:
SWEET

Alsace Sélection de Grains Nobles
concentrated and lingering notes

ORIGIN: FRANCE
Alsace

VARIETALS

COLOR

 Gewürztraminer pinot gris

 riesling muscat

AROMAS

yellow peach   apricot   exotic fruit

citrus fruits   candied fruit   honey

MOUTHFEEL

Alcohol Heat

1	5	10

Acidity Crispness

1	5	10

Sugar Sweetness

1	5	10

SERVE AT 46-50°F **COST** $$ or $$$

BEST TIME TO DRINK

1 year	5 years	10 years

FOOD PAIRINGS

 foie gras   blue cheese

 yellow fruit desserts   chocolate desserts

YOU MIGHT ALSO LIKE

late harvest Alsatian wine, German Riesling Trockenbeerenauslese, Quarts de Chaume, Bonnezeaux, Sauternes

---

Alsace Vendanges Tardives (late harvest)
rich and aromatic

ORIGIN: FRANCE
Alsace

VARIETALS

COLOR

riesling   Gewürztraminer

pinot gris   muscat

AROMAS

exotic fruit   yellow peach   citrus fruits

candied fruit   honey

MOUTHFEEL

Alcohol Heat

1	5	10

Acidity Crispness

1	5	10

Sugar Sweetness

1	5	10

SERVE AT 46-50°F **COST** $$$

BEST TIME TO DRINK

1 year	5 years	10 yea

FOOD PAIRINGS

 foie gras   Chinese cuisine

 Middle Eastern cuisine   washed rind cheese

 blue cheese   yellow fruit desserts

YOU MIGHT ALSO LIKE

Alsace sélection de grain nobles (selection of noble grapes), German Riesling Beerenauslese or Trockenbeerenauslese, Quarts de Chaume, Sauternes

Coteaux du Layon
unctuous and crisp

ORIGIN: FRANCE
Loire Valley (Anjou and Saumur)

VARIETALS **COLOR**

chenin

AROMAS

white flowers

citrus fruits

pear

yellow peach

apricot

quince

honey

exotic fruit

MOUTHFEEL

Alcohol Heat

1	5	10

Acidity Crispness

1	5	10

Sugar Sweetness

1	5	10

SERVE AT 46–50°F **COST** $$ to $$$

BEST TIME TO DRINK

1 year	10 years	20 years

FOOD PAIRINGS

foie gras

fish with sauce

Chinese cuisine

washed rind cheese

blue cheese

yellow fruits dessert

YOU MIGHT ALSO LIKE
Coteaux de l'Aubance, Bonnezeaux, Quarts de Chaume, semi-sweet Montlouis-sur-Loire, semi-sweet Vouvray, Coteaux de Saumur, Anjou Coteaux de la Loire

Ice Wine
pure and intense

ORIGIN: CANADA
Ontario

VARIETALS **COLOR**

riesling vidal

AROMAS

citronella

citrus fruits

candied fruit

honey

MOUTHFEEL

Alcohol Heat

1	5	10

Acidity Crispness

1	5	10

Sugar Sweetness

1	5	10

SERVE AT 45–50°F **COST** $$$$ to $$$$$$

BEST TIME TO DRINK

1 year	20 years	40 years

FOOD PAIRINGS

yellow fruit desserts white fruit desserts

aperitif

YOU MIGHT ALSO LIKE
sweet Riesling from Mosel and Rheingau (Eiswein, TBA), Alsace Riesling sélection de grains nobles

Jurançon Doux
concentrated and bright

ORIGIN: FRANCE
Southwest

VARIETALS

 petit manseng gros manseng

COLOR

AROMAS

 honey   white flowers   yellow peach

citrus fruits   exotic fruit   cinnamon

hazelnut

MOUTHFEEL

Alcohol Heat

1				5					10

Acidity Crispness

1				5					10

Sugar Sweetness

1				5					10

SERVE AT 46-50°F COST $$

BEST TIME TO DRINK

1 year			10 years				20 years

FOOD PAIRINGS

foie gras   poultry

pressed cheese   yellow fruit desserts

custardy desserts

YOU MIGHT ALSO LIKE

Pacherenc du Vic-Bilh, Sauternes, Monbazillac, Coteaux du Layon, late harvest Alsatian wine

---

Monbazillac
powerful and unctuous

ORIGIN: FRANCE
Southwest

VARIETALS

sémillon   sauvignon   muscadelle

COLOR

AROMAS

white flowers   apricot   honey

almond   hazelnut   vanilla

MOUTHFEEL

Alcohol Heat

1				5					10

Acidity Crispness

1				5					10

Sugar Sweetness

1				5					10

SERVE AT 46-50°F COST $$

BEST TIME TO DRINK

1 year			5 years					10 years

FOOD PAIRINGS

foie gras   poultry

white meat   custardy desserts

yellow fruit desserts

YOU MIGHT ALSO LIKE

Saussignac, sweet Côtes de Duras, Sainte-Croix-du-Mont, Cadillac, Loupiac, Sauternes, Barsac, Cérons

Moscato di Pantelleria

concentrated and middle eastern

ORIGIN: ITALY

Sicily and surrounding islands

VARIETALS

Zibibbo (Muscat of Alexandria)

COLOR

AROMAS

 raisin   candied fruit   candied orange

honey   quince

MOUTHFEEL

Alcohol Heat

1	5	10

Acidity Crispness

1	5	10

Sugar Sweetness

1	5	10

SERVE AT 50-55°F   **COST** $$ to $$$$

BEST TIME TO DRINK

1 year	10 years	20 years

FOOD PAIRINGS

blue cheese   yellow fruit desserts

aperitif

YOU MIGHT ALSO LIKE

Muscat du Cap Corse, Muscat de Beaumes de Venise, Muscat de Rivesaltes, Muscat de Samos

---

Muscat of Samos

rich and aromatic

ORIGIN: GREECE

Samos (Cyclades)

VARIETALS

 Muscat Blanc à Petits Grains

COLOR

AROMAS

white grape   exotic fruit   apricot

citrus fruits   white flowers   quince

honey

MOUTHFEEL

Alcohol Heat

1	5	10

Acidity Crispness

1	5	10

Sugar Sweetness

1	5	10

SERVE AT 46-50°F   **COST** $$

BEST TIME TO DRINK

1 year	5 years	10 years

FOOD PAIRINGS

aperitif   yellow fruit desserts

white fruit desserts

YOU MIGHT ALSO LIKE

Muscat du Cap Corse, Muscato (Passito di Pantelleria), Muscat de Beaumes de Venise, Muscat de Rivesaltes

Moscato
(California)
opulent and fragrant

ORIGIN: UNITED STATES
California

VARIETALS   **COLOR**

 muscat

AROMAS

 yellow peach   orange zest   white flowers

rose   exotic fruit

MOUTHFEEL

Alcohol Heat
| 1 | | | 5 | | | | 10 |

Acidity Crispness
| 1 | | | 5 | | | | 10 |

Sugar Sweetness
| 1 | | | 5 | | | | 10 |

SERVE AT 45-48°F   **COST** $ to $$$

BEST TIME TO DRINK
| 1 year | | 5 years | | | 10 years |

FOOD PAIRINGS

aperitif   yellow fruit desserts

YOU MIGHT ALSO LIKE
late harvest Alsace Muscat, Moscato d'Asti

Muscats doux
(Rivesaltes, Frontignan, Mireval, Saint-Jean-de-Minervois, Beaumes de Venise, Cap Corse)
smooth and aromatic

ORIGIN: FRANCE
Languedoc-Roussillon, Corsica, Rhône

VARIETALS   **COLOR**

 muscats

AROMAS

white flowers   rose   exotic fruit

citrus fruits   mint

MOUTHFEEL

Alcohol Heat
| 1 | | | 5 | | | | 10 |

Acidity Crispness
| 1 | | | 5 | | | | 10 |

Sugar Sweetness
| 1 | | | 5 | | | | 10 |

SERVE AT 46-50°F   **COST** $$

BEST TIME TO DRINK
| 1 year | | 5 years | | | 10 yea |

FOOD PAIRINGS

aperitif   Middle Eastern cuisine

custardy desserts   yellow fruit desserts

desserts with red fruit

YOU MIGHT ALSO LIKE
Muscat de Samos, Moscatel (Valencia), late harvest Alsace Muscat, Muscato (Passito di Pantelleria)

Montilla-Moriles P.X.
concentrated and complex

ORIGIN: SPAIN
Andalusia

VARIETALS
Pedro
Ximénez

COLOR

AROMAS

 honey   raisin   candied fruit

caramel   apricot

MOUTHFEEL

Alcohol Heat

1	5	10

Acidity Crispness

1	5	10

Sugar Sweetness

1	5	10

SERVE AT 50-54°F   **COST** $$ to $$$

BEST TIME TO DRINK

1 year	50 years	100 years

FOOD PAIRINGS

yellow fruit desserts   chocolate desserts

YOU MIGHT ALSO LIKE

Recioto Della Valpolicella, Vino Santo, Muscat de Samos, Muscato (Passito di Pantelleria)

Riesling Demi-Sec
delicate and decadent

ORIGIN: GERMANY
Mosel, Rheingau

VARIETALS
riesling

COLOR

AROMAS

 citrus fruits   apple   white flowers

apricot   yellow peach   minerality

smoked

MOUTHFEEL

Alcohol Heat

1	5	10

Acidity Crispness

1	5	10

Sugar Sweetness

1	5	10

SERVE AT 45-48°F   **COST** $$ to $$$$

BEST TIME TO DRINK

1 year	5 years	10 years

FOOD PAIRINGS

aperitif

YOU MIGHT ALSO LIKE

Vouvray, Montlouis-sur-Loire, Coteaux du Layon, Coteaux de l'Aubance

Riesling (Mosel)
bright and intense

ORIGIN: GERMANY
Mosel

....

VARIETALS   **COLOR**

 riesling

....

AROMAS

 citrus fruits   candied fruit   yellow peach

apricot   honey   mushrooms

minerality

....

MOUTHFEEL

Alcohol Heat

| 1 | | | | 5 | | | | | 10 |

Acidity Crispness

| 1 | | | | 5 | | | | | 10 |

Sugar Sweetness

| 1 | | | | 5 | | | | | 10 |

....

SERVE AT 46–50°F   **COST** $$ to $$$$

BEST TIME TO DRINK

| 1 year | 10 years | 20 years | 30 years | 40 years | 50 years |

....

FOOD PAIRINGS

aperitif   Indian cuisine

yellow fruit desserts   white fruit desserts

....

YOU MIGHT ALSO LIKE

late harvest and sélection de grains nobles Alsace Riesling, Jurançon Doux

Sauternes
powerful and complex

ORIGIN: FRANCE
Bordeaux (regions producing dessert wines)

....

VARIETALS   **COLOR**

sémillon   sauvignon   muscadelle

....

AROMAS

white flowers   citrus fruits   yellow peach

apricot   quince   honey

vanilla   toast

....

MOUTHFEEL

Alcohol Heat

| 1 | | | | 5 | | | | | 10 |

Acidity Crispness

| 1 | | | | 5 | | | | | 10 |

Sugar Sweetness

| 1 | | | | 5 | | | | | 10 |

....

SERVE AT 46–50°F   **COST** $$$ to $$$$

BEST TIME TO DRINK

| 1 year | 10 years | 20 years | 30 years | 40 years | 50 years |

....

FOOD PAIRINGS

foie gras   white meat

poultry   Chinese cuisine

fish with sauce   blue cheese

....

YOU MIGHT ALSO LIKE

Barsac, Cadillac, Sainte-Croix-du-Mont, Loupiac, Monbazillac

Tokaj
concentrated and complex

ORIGIN: HUNGARY
Tokaj

VARIETALS

COLOR

furmint   hársevelü

sárga
muskotály

AROMAS

apricot   citrus fruits   honey

candied
fruit   raisin   cinnamon

mushrooms

MOUTHFEEL

Alcohol Heat

1	5	10

Acidity Crispness

1	5	10

Sugar Sweetness

1	5	10

SERVE AT 50-54°F   **COST** $$ to $$$$

BEST TIME TO DRINK

1 year	50 years	100 years

FOOD PAIRINGS

foie gras   yellow fruit desserts

white fruit desserts   blue cheese

YOU MIGHT ALSO LIKE

Sauternes, Bonnezeaux, Alsace sélection de grain
nobles (selection of noble grapes), semi-sweet
Burgenland wine, Riesling Trockenbeerenauelese

Vin Santo
complex and lush

ORIGIN: ITALY
Tuscany

VARIETALS

COLOR

trebbiano   Malvasia

AROMAS

dried fruit   candied
fruit   honey

candied
orange   orange zest

MOUTHFEEL

Alcohol Heat

1	5	10

Acidity Crispness

1	5	10

Sugar Sweetness

1	5	10

SERVE AT 50-55°F   **COST** $$$ to $$$$$$

BEST TIME TO DRINK

1 year	10 years	20 years

FOOD PAIRINGS

blue cheese   yellow fruit desserts

aperitif   custardy desserts

YOU MIGHT ALSO LIKE

Jurançon, Gaillac Doux, Vin de Paille (Jura)

Vins Doux Naturels Ambrés
(Rivesaltes, Maury, Rasteau)
ripe and complex

ORIGIN: FRANCE

Languedoc-Roussillon and Rhone River Valley

VARIETALS

 grenache blanc

 grenache gris

COLOR

Macabeu

AROMAS

 apricot

quince

citrus fruits

candied fruit

almond

walnut

coffee

cinnamon

MOUTHFEEL

Alcohol Heat

1	5	10

Acidity Crispness

1	5	10

Sugar Sweetness

1	5	10

SERVE AT 50–54°F **COST** $$

BEST TIME TO DRINK

1 year	10 years	20 years	30 years	40 years

FOOD PAIRINGS

 aperitif

foie gras

 Chinese cuisine

Middle Eastern cuisine

 blue cheese

custardy desserts

YOU MIGHT ALSO LIKE

Tawny Port, Madère

Vouvray and Montlouis Moelleux
sweet and fresh

ORIGIN: FRANCE

Loire Valley (Touraine)

VARIETALS

 chenin

COLOR

AROMAS

white flowers

apple

pear

quince

candied fruit

honey

MOUTHFEEL

Alcohol Heat

1	5	10

Acidity Crispness

1	5	10

Sugar Sweetness

1	5	10

SERVE AT 46–50°F **COST** $$

BEST TIME TO DRINK

1 year	5 years	10 year

FOOD PAIRINGS

 foie gras

 Chinese cuisine

washed rind cheese

 yellow fruit desserts

YOU MIGHT ALSO LIKE

Coteaux du Layon, Coteaux de l'Aubance, Bonnezeaux, Quarts de Chaume, Anjou Coteaux de la Loire, Chenin Blanc (South Africa)

Also available in:

- semi-dry white
- dry white
- sparkling white

SPARKLING
WINES

Asti
sweet and Muscat-like

ORIGIN: ITALY
Piedmont

VARIETALS
 Muscat Blanc à Petits Grains

COLOR

AROMAS
 white flowers · rose · exotic fruit
citrus fruits · white grape

MOUTHFEEL

Alcohol Heat

1	5	10

Acidity Crispness

1	5	10

Sugar Sweetness

1	5	10

SERVE AT 45–46°F **COST** $$

BEST TIME TO DRINK

1 year	5 years	10 years

FOOD PAIRINGS
 white fruit desserts · citrus fruits
aperitif · yellow fruit desserts

YOU MIGHT ALSO LIKE

Clairette de Die, Blanquette de Limoux, Gaillac method wine, Crémant Demi-Sec, Moscato d'Asti, Champagne Demi-Sec

---

Cap Classique (South Africa)
round and fresh

ORIGIN: SOUTH AFRICA

VARIETALS
 pinot noir · chardonnay

COLOR

AROMAS
 citrus fruits · yellow peach · brioche
 white flowers · dried fruit

MOUTHFEEL

Alcohol Heat

1	5	10

Acidity Crispness

1	5	10

SERVE AT 45–46°F **COST** $$ to $$$

BEST TIME TO DRINK

1 year	5 years	10 years

FOOD PAIRINGS
 aperitif · grilled fish
 quiches and savory tarts · shellfish

YOU MIGHT ALSO LIKE

dry Champagne, Crémant, Franciacorta, Estate Method Traditionnelle Sparkling (Marlborough, Yarra Valley), Cap Classique

Cava
soft and light

ORIGIN: SPAIN
Catalonia

VARIETALS　　　　　　**COLOR**

 xarello　　Macabeo　　parellada

chardonnay

AROMAS

apple　　　pear　　　yellow peach

white flowers

MOUTHFEEL

Alcohol Heat

1				5					10

Acidity Crispness

1				5					10

SERVE AT 46–50°F　**COST** $

BEST TIME TO DRINK

1 year		5 years			10 years

FOOD PAIRINGS

 aperitif　　　　crustaceans (small)

grilled fish　　　　quiches and savory tarts

YOU MIGHT ALSO LIKE
NV Champagne, Crémant, Prosecco

Champagne (Blanc de blancs)
lively and fresh

ORIGIN: FRANCE
Champagne

VARIETALS　　　　　　**COLOR**

 chardonnay

AROMAS

white flowers　　white peach　　citrus fruits

butter　　　toast

MOUTHFEEL

Alcohol Heat

1				5					10

Acidity Crispness

1				5					10

SERVE AT 46–50°F　**COST** $$$ to $$$$$

BEST TIME TO DRINK

1 year		5 years			10 years

FOOD PAIRINGS

aperitif　　　　oysters

crustaceans (small)　　scallops

white meat　　　grilled fish

YOU MIGHT ALSO LIKE
Crémant de Bourgogne, Crémant du Jura, Crémant d'Alsace, Crémant de Limoux Blanc de Blancs

Also available in:
 rosé

201

Champagne Brut and Extra-Brut
lively and intense

ORIGIN: FRANCE
Champagne

VARIETALS

 pinot noir
pinot meunier

COLOR
 chardonnay

AROMAS

white flowers

citrus fruits

yellow peach

brioche

MOUTHFEEL

Alcohol Heat

| 1 | | 5 | | 10 |

Acidity Crispness

| 1 | | 5 | | 10 |

SERVE AT 46–50°F **COST** $$$ to $$$$$

BEST TIME TO DRINK

| 1 year | | 5 years | | 10 years |

FOOD PAIRINGS

 aperitif   oysters

crustaceans (small)   scallops

fish with sauce   poultry

YOU MIGHT ALSO LIKE

Crémant de Bourgogne, Crémant du Jura, Crémant d'Alsace, Crémant de Limoux and other regional Crémants

Rosé Champagne (Brut)
fresh and fruity

ORIGIN: FRANCE
Champagne

VARIETALS

 pinot noir
 pinot meunier

COLOR
 chardonnay

AROMAS

 cherry   strawberry   raspberry

blackcurrant

MOUTHFEEL

Alcohol Heat

| 1 | | 5 | | 10 |

Acidity Crispness

| 1 | | 5 | | 10 |

SERVE AT 46–50°F **COST** $$$ to $$$$$

BEST TIME TO DRINK

| 1 year | | 5 years | | 10 years |

FOOD PAIRINGS

 aperitif   poultry

 white meat   crustaceans (small)

desserts with red fruit   chocolate desserts

YOU MIGHT ALSO LIKE

Crémant d'Alsace, Crémant de Bourgogne, Rosés and other sparkling rosés made with Pinot Noir

Also available in:
 rosé

Cremants
bright and fruity

ORIGIN: FRANCE
Alsace, Burgundy, Loire, Jura, Limoux, Bordeaux, Luxembourg

VARIETALS

 chardonnay   pinot noir   pinot blanc

chenin   cabernets

COLOR

AROMAS

white flowers   citrus fruits   white peach

apple

MOUTHFEEL

Alcohol Heat

1	5	10

Acidity Crispness

1	5	10

SERVE AT 46-50°F **COST** $

BEST TIME TO DRINK

1 year	5 years	10 years

FOOD PAIRINGS

aperitif   oysters

scallops   grilled fish

fish with sauce   white meat

YOU MIGHT ALSO LIKE
NV Champagne, Saumur, Vouvray, Montlouis-sur-Loire, Prosecco

German Sekt
fresh and lively

ORIGIN: GERMANY

VARIETALS

riesling   müller-thurgau   pinot blanc

pinot gris

COLOR

AROMAS

citrus fruits   white flowers   pear

minerality

MOUTHFEEL

Alcohol Heat

1	5	10

Acidity Crispness

1	5	10

SERVE AT 45-46°F **COST** $ to $$

BEST TIME TO DRINK

1 year	5 years	10 years

FOOD PAIRINGS

aperitif   crustaceans (small)

pressed cheese   shellfish

grilled fish   sushi, raw fish

YOU MIGHT ALSO LIKE
Cava, Prosecco, Crémant

Also available in:
● rosé

Also available in:
● rosé

Franciacorta
fine with finesse

ORIGIN: ITALY
Lombardy

VARIETALS

COLOR

chardonnay pinot noir

AROMAS

citrus fruits white flowers brioche

grilled yellow peach

MOUTHFEEL

Alcohol Heat

1	5	10

Acidity Crispness

1	5	10

SERVE AT 45–48°F **COST** $$ to $$$$$

BEST TIME TO DRINK

1 year	5 years	10 years

FOOD PAIRINGS

aperitif scallops

crustaceans (small)

YOU MIGHT ALSO LIKE

Franciacorta, dry Champagne, Estate Methode Traditionnelle Sparkling (Marlborough, Yarra Valley, Cap Classique), Cava

---

Also available in:
rosé

Sweet Lambrusco
fruity and decadent

ORIGIN: ITALY
Emilia-Romagna

VARIETALS

COLOR

lambrusco

AROMAS

strawberry raspberry red currants

blackcurrant

MOUTHFEEL

Tannins Firmness

1	5	10

Alcohol Heat

1	5	10

Acidity Crispness

1	5	10

Sugar Sweetness

1	5	10

SERVE AT 46–50°F **COST** $

BEST TIME TO DRINK

1 year	5 years	10 years

FOOD PAIRINGS

aperitif desserts with red fruit

charcuterie

YOU MIGHT ALSO LIKE

Sparkling Reds (Loire Valley), Sparling Shiraz, Sparkling Red Burgundy

---

Also available in:
rosé

Moscato d'Asti
decadent and fruity

ORIGIN: ITALY
Piedmont

VARIETALS
 Muscat Blanc à Petits Grains

COLOR

AROMAS
 white flowers

 white grape

exotic fruit

yellow peach

citronella

orange zest

 honey

MOUTHFEEL
Alcohol Heat

1	5	10

Acidity Crispness

1	5	10

Sugar Sweetness

1	5	10

SERVE AT 45-46°F COST $ to $$

BEST TIME TO DRINK

1 year	5 years	10 years

FOOD PAIRINGS
 aperitif

 yellow fruit desserts

 white fruit desserts

YOU MIGHT ALSO LIKE
Clairette de Die, Blanquette de Limoux, Gaillac method wine, Crémant Doux, Asti

---

Prosecco Brut
light and fragrant

ORIGIN: ITALY
Veneto

VARIETALS
 glera

COLOR

AROMAS
white flowers

 apple

 white peach

pear

MOUTHFEEL
Alcohol Heat

1	5	10

Acidity Crispness

1	5	10

SERVE AT 46-50°F COST $

BEST TIME TO DRINK

1 year	5 years	10 years

FOOD PAIRINGS
aperitif

crustaceans (small)

grilled fish

quiches and savory tarts

YOU MIGHT ALSO LIKE
NV Champagne, Crémant, Saumur, Cava, Gaillac

Prosecco
supple and decadent

ORIGIN: ITALY
Veneto

VARIETALS
 glera

COLOR

AROMAS
 white flowers

apple

white peach

pear

MOUTHFEEL
Alcohol Heat

1	5	10

Acidity Crispness

1	5	10

Sugar Sweetness

1	5	10

SERVE AT 45-48°F **COST** $ to $$

BEST TIME TO DRINK

1 year	5 years	10 years

FOOD PAIRINGS
 aperitif

yellow fruit desserts

 white fruit desserts

YOU MIGHT ALSO LIKE

Clairette de Die, Blanquette de Limoux, Gaillac method wine, Crémant Demi-Sec

Sparkling Saumur
light and fresh

ORIGIN: FRANCE
Loire Valley (Anjou and Saumur)

VARIETALS
chenin

COLOR

AROMAS
white flowers

yellow peach

pear

MOUTHFEEL
Alcohol Heat

1	5	10

Acidity Crispness

1	5	10

SERVE AT 46-50°F **COST** $

BEST TIME TO DRINK

1 year	5 years	10 years

FOOD PAIRINGS
 aperitif

 oysters

 white meat

 poultry

 quiches and savory tarts

 fish with sauce

YOU MIGHT ALSO LIKE

Vouvray, Montlouis-sur-Loire, Crémant de Loire and other regional Crémants, Champagne

Also available in:
● rosé

Champagne-style Wines (Australia)
soft and fresh

ORIGIN: AUSTRALIA
Victoria

VARIETALS **COLOR**
 chardonnay pinot noir

AROMAS
yellow peach   citrus fruits   white flowers
hazelnut   brioche

MOUTHFEEL
Alcohol Heat

1	5	10

Acidity Crispness

1	5	10

SERVE AT 45–48°F   **COST** $$$

BEST TIME TO DRINK

1 year	5 years	10 years

FOOD PAIRINGS
aperitif   quiches and savory tarts
poultry   grilled fish
sushi, raw fish

YOU MIGHT ALSO LIKE
Franciacorta, dry Champagne, Estate Methode Traditionnelle Sparkling (Russian River Valley), Estate Methode Traditionnelle Sparkling Cap Classique

Also available in:
● rosé

Champagne-style Wines (California)
refined and fresh

ORIGIN: UNITED STATES
California

VARIETALS **COLOR**
chardonnay pinot noir

AROMAS
citrus fruits   white flowers   hazelnut
butter   toast   yellow peach

MOUTHFEEL
Alcohol Heat

1	5	10

Acidity Crispness

1	5	10

SERVE AT 46–52°F   **COST** $$ to $$$

BEST TIME TO DRINK

1 year	5 years	10 years

FOOD PAIRINGS
aperitif   scallops
white meat   fish with sauce

YOU MIGHT ALSO LIKE
dry Champagne, Cava, Crémant, Franciacorta

Also available in:
● rosé

Sparkling Shiraz
unexpected and tasty

ORIGIN: AUSTRALIA

VARIETALS

 syrah/shiraz

COLOR

AROMAS

 black fruit jam

 smoked

spices

cacao

blackcurrant

leather

MOUTHFEEL

Tannins Firmness

1	5	10

Alcohol Heat

1	5	10

Acidity Crispness

1	5	10

Sugar Sweetness

1	5	10

SERVE AT 50-55°F COST $$

BEST TIME TO DRINK

1 year	5 years	10 years

FOOD PAIRINGS

 aperitif

 chocolate dessert

 desserts with red fruit

 barbecue

 Chinese cuisine

YOU MIGHT ALSO LIKE

Lambrusco

APPENDICES

PICTOGRAMS: KEY

WINE AROMAS

 apricot

 citrus fruits

 almond

 pineapple

 anise

 butter

 wood

 fruit candy

 brioche

 firewood

 cacao

 coffee

 cinnamon

 caramel

 blackcurrant

 black cherry

 cherry

 mushrooms

 lemon

 clove

 quince

 black fruit jam

 red fruit jam

 leather

 spices

 fig

 white flowers

 hay

 strawberry

 raspberry

 candied fruit

 exotic fruit

 dried fruit

 smoked

 scrubland

 game

 ginger

 grilled

Morello cherry

red currants

green herbs

mango

melon

mint

honey

minerality

mocha

blackberry

blueberry

hazelnut

walnut

black olive

orange

candied orange

toast

grapefruit

white peach

yellow peach

TYPES OF FOOD FOR PAIRING

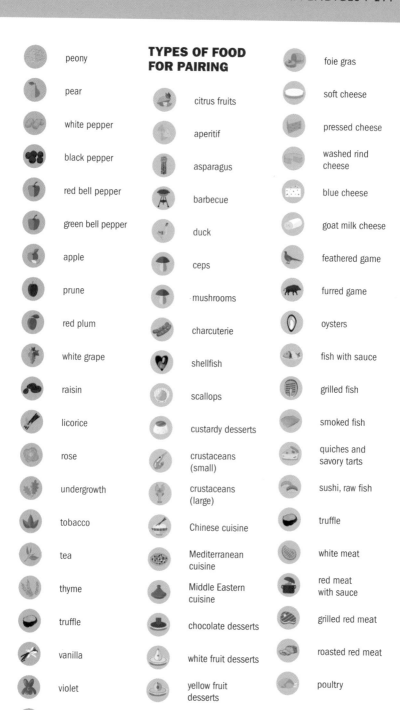

peony

pear

white pepper

black pepper

red bell pepper

green bell pepper

apple

prune

red plum

white grape

raisin

licorice

rose

undergrowth

tobacco

tea

thyme

truffle

vanilla

violet

orange zest

citrus fruits

aperitif

asparagus

barbecue

duck

ceps

mushrooms

charcuterie

shellfish

scallops

custardy desserts

crustaceans (small)

crustaceans (large)

Chinese cuisine

Mediterranean cuisine

Middle Eastern cuisine

chocolate desserts

white fruit desserts

yellow fruit desserts

desserts with red fruit

foie gras

soft cheese

pressed cheese

washed rind cheese

blue cheese

goat milk cheese

feathered game

furred game

oysters

fish with sauce

grilled fish

smoked fish

quiches and savory tarts

sushi, raw fish

truffle

white meat

red meat with sauce

grilled red meat

roasted red meat

poultry

INDEX

THE APPELLATIONS

The page numbers in bold refer to descriptions devoted to the wine.

INDEX OF WINE AROMAS

NOTES

NOTES

NOTES

Director, Hachette Pratique: Catherine Saunier-Talec

Project Director: Stéphane Rosa

Editors: Juliette de Lavaur, Christine Cuperly et Audrey Di-Santo

Editorial collaboration: Sébastien Durand-Viel

Art Director: Antoine Béon

Graphic Design & Illustration: Jess Grinneiser

Manufacturing: Isabelle Simon-Bourg

Composition and photoengraving: Nord Compo

Translated from French by Carmella Abramowitz Moreau

First published in the United States of America in 2018 by

Universe Publishing, a division of

Rizzoli International Publications, Inc.

300 Park Avenue South

New York, NY 10010

www.rizzoliusa.com

Originally published in French in 2016 by

Hachette Livre

© 2016 Hachette Livre (Hachette Pratique)

2018 2019 2020 2021 / 10 9 8 7 6 5 4 3 2 1

ISBN: 978-0-7893-3446-6

Library of Congress Control Number: 2018945341

Printed in China